The
Recovery
Toolkit

A 12 week plan to support your journey
from Domestic Abuse

Sue Penna

The Author of *The Recovery Toolkit* Group Programme

First published in 2020 by Penna & Passmore Ltd

ISBN 978-1-8380250-0-7

Penna & Passmore Ltd

Contents

Comments from participants who attended the 12 week Recovery Toolkit programme

Attending the Recovery Toolkit programme was an incredible experience and was so valuable to me. The most useful thing was learning to understand and accept I was abused, and I was not responsible for it. The programme also taught me that there was a life after abuse. Since attending I no longer feel ashamed of my past. I'm socially more confident and I am generally less anxious about going out and meeting new people. **G.A.**

I feel able to be more open with my children and I can now be a better role model for them. I cannot recommend this course enough and urge anyone who has gone through domestic abuse to go for it! It will change your life! **N.K.**

It's all about healing yourself and building yourself up now that you understand what has happened in your relationship. It allows you to wear your heart on your sleeve, be open without feeling you are being judged. It's a 'warts and all' acceptance of ourselves and how to move forward with all our various bits of baggage. **Stephanie**

This was a programme that was all about me and building me up. It was not long before I started to remember who I was and my discovering a new, stronger me. Over the weeks I felt myself getting stronger. I was no longer a victim, I was a survivor and a women, fighting to get back to who she used to be. The confidence I found was something I'd previously only ever dreamed of. I cannot recommend The Recovery Toolkit enough. It gives you confidence, support and strength. It also makes you realise that not only are you worth it, but you are beautiful! So, the message from one survivor (me) to every other survivor thinking of doing The Recovery Toolkit, find the strength because you are beautiful and most definitely worth it! Good luck and believe in yourself. **L.C.**

This has been one of the most life-affirming and supportive experiences I have ever had. The course helped me understand my experience and believe that there will be love, joy and hope for my life moving forward. **Eleanor.**

Attending the Recovery Toolkit programme was enlightening, empowering and overall an amazing experience! I wish you all well and that you gain the strength and knowledge you need to go on to a wonderful life! xx **Edwina.**

You're on the right road to getting yourself back to who you want to be. The programme gave me the confidence and understanding of the abuse I suffered and the fact it was not my fault. You can do this too!
Keep going, believe in yourself and be YOU! xx **L.B.**

The Recovery Toolkit has helped me complete my journey, back to finding myself and to feeling stronger. I advise you to complete each week. You will gain so much and feel supported. This is an invaluable course, it is so informative and empowering. Your confidence grows over the weeks. I really recommend it! **L.S.**

The course has been an incredible experience and I would recommend it to anyone who has lived with domestic abuse, who is now healing and building a new future. It has given me invaluable support and new skills that I will take forward. It has not only changed my life but that of my children's too. I am now positive and excited for the future while having a new awareness that it all takes time. **E.N.**

The Recovery Toolkit has helped me to move on with my life positively. It has been educational, enlightening, empowering and invaluably supportive. It has also helped me discover where I have been, and where I want to be going. It's helped me really look at who I was, who I've become and who I want to be. My life has completely turned around since being on the course! I shall always be so grateful. I have become braver, stronger and feel more like myself. I am so pleased that I stuck with it! As a result, my children are also doing so much better. **Nina**

The Recovery Toolkit is the most inspiring, informative, course. It will empower women even more with a continued, deeper, in-depth knowledge, awareness and understanding of the perpetrator's mind and tactics. It has more 'aha', light bulb moments, more in-depth understanding of the psychology of the perpetrator's mind, and the control and manipulative tactics they use. **Mel**

This course has taught me how to stand up for myself and how to say no! I now know I have the right to be respected, to be myself, to go out, have a friend and be strong etc **S.N.**

The Recovery Toolkit has been invaluable in helping me move on and find a way to rebuild my self-esteem and to like myself again. I am now proud to be me. **Linda B.**

This time last year I was five months out of detox and struggled to leave the house. I was fearful my ex would try and find us and it was a constant trigger to my complex PTSD, which was diagnosed as a direct result of the abuse. People have often said to me 'you know how to pick them, don't you?' I used to nod and feel ashamed and stupid. Now I say "No. They pick me. My mind isn't wired like theirs, so I never stood a chance!" How could I ever have known the signs, recognised their narcissistic intentions, seen through their charming words and promises of true love, and my being the best person that they had ever known? **Sheila L.**

My confidence and humour have returned and I am so happy at work with my new colleagues and clients. The programme has given me my mind back and has freed me of the guilt and shame I was carrying as a mother and usually intelligent woman. I am so grateful. After attending the Recovery Toolkit programme has helped me to find myself. In lots of ways, my confidence has grown. Attending the course has been the start of a new chapter in my life. After years of feeling worthless, I am finally discovering myself again. My advice to those following the programme is that you can and will feel free again. Keep going, be strong, you're worth it. **E.R.**

I would say that doing the Domestic Abuse Recovery Toolkit programme is the best thing I could have done. It has helped me gain insight into and a perspective of my previous abusive relationship. It has also helped my children, as my behaviour towards them has changed for the better. I am now feeling positive for the future because I engaged in this programme. **Karen L.**

Since attending the Recovery Toolkit programme I've noticed a very positive change in my thought processes. This change enables me to look within myself for the answers that otherwise I would have sought elsewhere. Such was my connection to my ex-partner it was my norm to engage with him albeit in a negative way. I was still trying to appease him and felt that his power was such that he had ultimate control over me. I now understand this was power I was giving him by not asserting myself in a healthier way. I am stronger and freer than I have been for the last decade. **Victoria S.**

The Recovery Toolkit programme has had a massive impact on my life. I now look forward to waking up each day and living my life the way I want to live it; happily, lovingly and with tremendous positivity. **Gerry B.**

Coming to the group has definitely helped me to realise that I am worth more than the abuse and treatment I had been receiving from my ex-husband. Life was very bleak but now I realise that there is a future out there for me to be happy again one day because I have learnt to love myself. This programme was well worth the commitment and has increased my confidence and improved my mental well being. **E.L.**

The Recovery Toolkit programme has given me the confidence and assertiveness that has been needed when dealing with abusive people within my life. It has also protected the lives of my younger children as I can teach them the coping strategies that I have learned to deal with negative people, situations, feelings and thoughts. **J.P.**

Simply put the Recovery Toolkit programme is life-changing. To realise you are not alone or deserving of the abuse is liberating. To have found so many wonderful, kind, caring and inspirational women who show such strength and determination after having faced so much is a blessing. To have found women who build each other up, support and nurture each other makes you realise there are good people in the world. **E.C.**

The Recovery Toolkit programme really does work. It actually changes you and the way you think. I was sceptical at first, but it has made such a massive difference to my life and my relationships. The facilitators are confident & passionate in their work and they support you throughout the programme. I would recommend this programme to anyone who has experienced an abusive relationship. **T.W.**

The Recovery Toolkit

A 12 week plan to support
your journey from Domestic Abuse

Preface

The Recovery Toolkit is inspired by and written for those individuals who have experienced being in a relationship with an abusive partner. The book explores some of the problems you may still encounter despite having separated from that relationship.

The information and observations contained in these pages aim to empower you to lead a life safe in the knowledge that you are no longer controlled or influenced by that earlier experience.

The book is also recommended reading for anyone working with those that have experienced domestic abuse. The Recovery Toolkit aims to give the reader an insight into the difficulties those that have experienced abuse have had to face to truly overcome the abusive legacy.

When I wrote the original programme, on which this book is based, I had no idea it would be so popular. Since its creation, the twelve-week course, called the Recovery Toolkit programme, has helped hundreds of participants and has drawn a huge amount of positive feedback from those that have taken part. Whilst for some people attending a group programme is ideal, it does not suit everyone and it may not be possible for you to attend, hence the book you hold in your hands.

The Recovery Toolkit book does not seek to replace the Recovery Toolkit programme, but it aims to provide the same knowledge and resulting empowerment to those who have experienced abusive relationships.

To quote George Orwell, "knowledge is power" and as the author of the programme and this book, I truly believe this. Empowerment, one of the aims of the book, is something that I hope you will benefit from.

Sue Penna 2020

WARNING!

This book and the plans it contains are only suitable for individuals who are no longer in an abusive relationship. If you are still in an abusive relationship this book is not for you as following the suggestions in these pages could result in you increasing the risk of harm to yourself and others.

This book is designed to empower those who read it, rebuild their self-confidence and help them to re-establish boundaries. Whilst these things are all positive, if you are still in an abusive relationship, your abusive partner may feel that they are losing their control over you which could escalate their abusive behaviours.

However, sometimes we know that separation doesn't mean never seeing the abuser again, through child contact arrangements, court cases and sometimes continued stalking and harassment the abuse can continue. In these situations, the book should help BUT if at any time you feel frightened or feel yourself to be in danger call the police on 999.

I've published a list of organisations at the end of the book who you can contact if you want help and they will signpost you to your local agencies.

Remember, if you feel you are in immediate danger dial 999.

Introduction

To start with, congratulations you are an amazing person. What? How can I say that as I have never met you? Well, you must have lived through some distressing times to pick up this book to browse or purchase it. There are many reasons why you have started to read these pages. It could be the nagging sense that what you experienced, still troubles you. You may still have some contact with your ex-partner through child contact or you may have no contact with them, either way, it is likely you still feel their influence and this stops you moving forward.

The very fact you are still trying to resolve what you have endured, whilst also trying to be the best person you can be for yourself and any children plus your family and friends, is the very reason why I think you're amazing! So please accept the praise. Remember, you are, by the very act of looking at this book, trying to change your life for the better.

Already, I can imagine that a voice in your head is telling you that I am talking rubbish! If only I knew you, if only I realised you are not amazing, if only I knew how useless you were, the mistakes you make. Is this a familiar response? If you've answered yes, then remember that answer as you work your way through the book.

Working with people who have experienced abusive relationships

I have always been struck by some of the statements I've heard them say: "What did, I do to cause this?" and "The cuts and bruises heal. What doesn't go away is their (the abusers) voice in my head." I was meeting individuals who had separated from abusive partners, some recently and others who had separated many years earlier, but they all still said these same things.

These statements confirmed what I had come to believe thanks to my background as an Occupational Therapist specialising in Mental Health in adult psychiatry and counselling; that it is almost impossible to experience abuse and it not have a continued impact on an individual's mental health after the relationship has ended.

Despite this, by the end of the book, I predict that you will be able to recognise, for yourself, how amazing you are! Reading this book can be a starting point for the rest of your life, it will potentially change the way you think, feel and behave. Most importantly, it is about being able to come back to the techniques in the future if doubts/old ways start to appear again.

That may be hard to believe, so in many ways, I am asking you to take a big leap of faith to work your way through this book. But I believe that if you follow the directions and practice the exercises, you will be thrilled and delighted at the changes you can make in 12 short weeks.

Survival Techniques

When we experience abuse, the strategies we adopt to cope with the abusive behaviour alter our perceptions of the world around us. The effort of meeting the abuser's demands and punishments in order to fight the fear they induce means you will have often developed many unconscious survival techniques.

I believe that there are techniques that can enable us to challenge and replace those we used while in the abusive relationship. These new replacement techniques are more suitable for the non-abusive world we now live in.

What I am suggesting is that to cope with the discrepancies in your former intimate relationship (such as the person who was supposed to love and cherish you being the one who hurt you most physically and/or emotionally) you will have made adjustments to the way you think that will have impacted on your core beliefs.

Once these core beliefs have been altered as a result of the abuse, your self-worth, self-esteem and self-confidence will have diminished. Even now, having left the abuser, you may experience mood swings, you may no longer know who to trust and indeed when you do trust people they may seem to let you down. When things go wrong you may still be convinced it is your fault.

You might be afraid to share personal details with others or you find yourself telling the same story about your life over and over again without ever feeling better about it.

You could find that drinking alcohol or taking drugs are the only ways you can cope with your see-sawing emotions. If you have children you may be overprotective and see danger everywhere for them. New relationships could have broken down to the extent that they seem to mirror the abuse you experienced with your partner.

You may have tried another relationship only to be abused again or you are currently in a relationship that is not abusive but you constantly expect it to fail as you are 'not good enough' for your new partner. Perhaps you avoid and fear intimacy with others, but because you still crave it you engage in risky sexual behaviour with strangers.

What To Do

You may recognise some or all of the feelings mentioned in the last few paragraphs. This book will give you a better understanding of why you may feel these things and it will suggest ways in which you can turn your thinking and emotions around.

This may sound like hard work and it will require that you follow the directions suggested and complete the worksheets or exercises, but I believe you will find doing so will be a turning point in your life.

Don't Rush – Listen to the voice that knows best, your own! Instead, take your time and read one chapter a week. Once you have read a chapter there are exercises and worksheets to complete. These can be done over the week as can re-reading the chapter to make sure you have understood what is written.

I can imagine that there is a sense of urgency, that you want to start to feel better as soon as possible, but to rush this process will not make it happen quicker.

The negative changes in your thought patterns may have taken several years to become your default behaviour (abusers are very patient), so respect yourself and give yourself time to understand and consolidate any changes.

This book sets out to teach you positive techniques you can use so that you can finally get rid of "the voice of the perpetrator in your head" and relearn how to listen to your voice, the voice that knows best for you.

Final comment – This is a starting point for the rest of your life. The following 12 weeks will potentially change the way you think, feel and behave, and it is important to remember that you will be able to come back to the techniques in the future if doubts/ old ways start to appear again. After potentially many years of abuse, it is likely that you will continue to experience some of the negative thinking at times, and that that is ok, but now you will have skills to deal with it more effectively.

JUST ONCE MORE

If you are still in an abusive relationship please go no further. Following this programme will change your attitudes and behaviour, and if you are still in an abusive relationship to do so could have very serious consequences.

There are twelve weekly chapters in this book. I suggest that you read one chapter a week and start at the same time and day each week if you can. For example, every Sunday at 7 pm. The most benefit will come from reading the chapters in order.

Jennifer Gilmour

Also included in the book are some observations by Jennifer Gilmour (JG), who after surviving and leaving an abusive relationship, took part in the programme the book is based on. Although it is not necessary to read Jennifer's anecdotes to follow the programme, I hope you'll find them an inspiring and useful addition.

As I have mentioned you may need to read the chapters more than once, and then you'll need to consider what the exercises are and how you are going to do them.

You can then spend the next week focusing on what you have read in the chapter, you may wish to go back and read it several times.

A Right To Privacy

During the twelve weeks, you will be writing down and recording information about your progress. You may want to think about where and how you are going to do this. You could buy a notebook to write in, or a ring binder file or even just use some scrap paper or the back of an envelope.

However you decide to record this information remember you may want to have somewhere private to keep it as it is for your eyes only. You may not have been used to having privacy in your abusive relationship and secrets were always unpleasant or painful. Neither of these are true in this situation. You have every right to privacy and this is not secretive it is personal and therefore does not have to be shared with anyone else.

Before you read further you need to decide when your regular reading time is going to be. Try to make sure you will have no interruptions during this time and have paper and pens handy. Each week you will be asked to complete some exercises that relate to the chapter you have read. As hard as it is to be disciplined to do this, it is vital to your benefitting from the programme laid out in this book.

Again, try and work out regular slots in the week when you will have uninterrupted time to really focus and therefore give yourself the attention you deserve.

Remember, one week, one chapter!

Good luck. The closer you follow the instructions and suggestions the more you will benefit.

An Abusive Relationship?

What do we mean by the term 'abusive relationship'? There is a range of experiences that can all be described as abusive in an intimate relationship. Generally, I use the term to depict a relationship where one person has to modify or change their behaviour, attitudes and thinking, to accommodate the wishes of another. Sometimes the person adapts just for a quiet life, sometimes because the consequences of noncompliance would be severe. All relationships tend to start well but the timescale as to how long the 'honeymoon' period lasts can vary from weeks to months. It can be almost impossible to spot the subtle changes that take place within the relationship which alter the power base so that it shifts from one of equality to one of abuse.

Isolation

Your partner may not have liked you seeing friends or family, often defending this position with what may seem a good reason - "they are not good enough for you", "they don't like me". They may have objected to your working or taking part in work social activities – "you don't need to work we have enough money", "why would you want to spend time with work colleagues when you have me at home?".

If you have children your partner may have prevented them from joining in extra school activities or social events – "the other children aren't good enough for our children", "we need to protect the children from bad influences".

It's hard to see the wood for the trees when we love someone and all of this can seem extremely reasonable. However, the net result of this is to isolate you from other people who might notice or comment on the power imbalance in your relationship and to make you more dependent on the abuser as you lose connections with the other people in your life.

Financial Control

Your partner may have suggested it would be easier to have a single bank account and for them to manage the finances. At first, this idea could have seemed (and be) a reasonable position.

16

However, if this leads to your having no access to money or being made to be accountable for every penny, the result is that you have lost control over your finances and you are therefore being controlled.

Unfortunately, by the time this happens so much will have been invested in the relationship that it can be easy to justify your partner's actions as 'overprotectiveness'.

In an abusive relationship, there is always one person who has control and coerces the other person to do what they want through the use of emotional blackmail, bullying techniques or threatening behaviour.

Ridicule

The abuse you suffered may have been more direct, putting you down, name-calling, ridiculing your clothes, hair, or your choice of TV show. It's sadly true that most of us are willing to believe the negative feedback we get from others.

Rather than rebut these comments we reflect inwardly and often try to change these things to make the other person love us more. We diet, change our hairstyle, dress differently and watch different TV shows.

We start to change our behaviour, to satisfy our partner, rather than be comfortable with how we are and challenge them to accept us and give us unconditional love. We adapt to a situation where we only receive love if we look and behave in a manner that complies with our partner's demands rather than that which makes us happy. This is control and abuse.

Threat

The abuse may have involved actual or perceived threats of physical violence. You didn't have to be assaulted to be abused. Someone threatening to hit you can be as controlling as actually being hit. Especially if you are aware they are capable of carrying out the threat.

They may also have threatened to take the children away from you, put pictures on social media, hurt pets, or tell people stories about you. The list is endless. If your partner used fear to intimidate you into changing or modifying your behaviour, this was abuse.

17

Sexual Abuse

Your partner may have put pressure on you to have sex with them whether or not you wanted to and in ways that you were uncomfortable with. They may have justified this by saying they have a higher sex drive, needed more variation to be stimulated or called you frigid or a prude if you tried to refuse their demands. They may have threatened to find someone else who would satisfy them or they flaunted affairs and sexual relationships with others, even bringing other individuals to the home.

This behaviour leaves us feeling humiliated and degraded and unfortunately, we are often made to feel it is our fault, that we are not sexy enough, desirable enough or adventurous enough.

Yet again, through no fault of our own, our self-esteem, confidence and general well-being plummet, either because we were forced to take part in sex against our will, or we were punished for not doing so. It is worth noting that rape in marriage became a criminal offence in 1991.

You may have heard the term 'domestic abuse' or 'domestic violence' and even though you were living with any or all the above scenarios you may not for a moment have imagined that this was what you were experiencing. You may have developed various practical and psychological mechanisms for coping with the situation you were in.

Some people suffer mental health problems, some turn to drink and drugs, others just shut down and try and accept the situation. Whatever you did, you are now out of that situation and you should applaud yourself for that.

A Definition Of Domestic Violence And Abuse

The UK Government definition [1] of domestic violence and abuse is any incident or pattern of incidents of controlling, coercive or threatening behaviour, violence or abuse between those aged 16 or over [2] who are or have been intimate partners or family members regardless of gender or sexuality. This can encompass, but is not limited to, the following types of abuse:

Psychological/Emotional
Examples include: ridicule, name calling, threatening, making you think you are to blame and going mad, humiliating.

Physical
Examples include: Pinching, hair pulling, spitting, beatings, slapping and burning.

Sexual
Examples include: forced sexual intercourse (rape), making you watch pornography.

Financial
Examples include: not allowing access to a bank account, running up debts in an abused persons name, insisting on receipts for everything,

Controlling behaviour is a range of acts designed to make a person subordinate and/or dependent by isolating them from sources of support, exploiting their resources and capacities for personal gain, depriving them of the means needed for independence, resistance and escape and regulating their everyday behaviour.

Coercive behaviour is an act or a pattern of acts of assault, threats, humiliation and intimidation or other abuse that is used to harm, punish, or frighten their victim.

In 2015, England and Wales became the first nations in the world to criminalise such controlling behaviour within relationships, making coercive control punishable by up to five years in jail.

The Government definition, which is not a legal definition, includes so-called 'honour' based violence, female genital mutilation (FGM) and forced marriage, and is clear that victims are not confined to one gender or ethnic group.

WEEK ONE
How We Think

For this first week, I am going to explain to you the theory behind the programme laid out in the pages of this book. I will also explain how you can use the information and exercises contained within its pages to enable you to overcome the effects on your thinking and the resulting behaviour that your abuser cultivated whilst you were in your former relationship.

What do I mean by that? Remember, you were living in an abusive relationship that forced you to develop coping strategies that have kept you and any children, safe within the confines of the abusive relationship. It was probably a relationship where you had little say as the power and controlling behaviour was undertaken by your ex-partner.

The psychological distress caused by the abuse you endured may still affect how you perceive yourself and cause you to have low self-esteem and poor self-worth. This distress will probably affect how you interact with other people. In fact, you may find that you have become more angry or passive in your relationships with others.

The stress of your former relationship is likely to have triggered negative responses in how you manage any emotional pain. Perhaps you are living with depression or anxiety or both. If so, you may misuse alcohol or drugs to feel better (self-medicating).

If you have children, the distress you felt within your former abusive relationship may have affected how you contributed to parenting those children. This will almost certainly be the case if those parenting skills were being sabotaged by your abuser.

The distress you endured may also have left you confused about issues of trust, boundaries and respectful relationships with adults and children including friends and family.

Whilst this book covers many of the issues that can still affect those who have experienced an abusive relationship, everyone reading these pages is an individual and will have particular needs and areas that they will want to concentrate on. For example, you may find that working on your self-esteem is the most important factor for you and that managing your anger is less of an issue. With that in mind, you may want to focus on the exercises that help to improve your self-esteem. It is worthwhile doing the exercises as it will help you to rid yourself of those negative patterns of thought and the negative behaviours you may be experiencing. You will gain the most from this book if you follow the outlined suggestions.

Be honest with yourself

One word of caution, there is a need to be mindful and to challenge yourself. This is especially important if while following the suggestions laid out in the book you start to focus on an area that is easy for you to work on whilst avoiding those areas that might be more difficult. It's up to you how honest you are with yourself! The weekly programme in this book is designed along what is called psycho-educational lines. Psycho-education? The term refers to the education offered to people who suffer from distress as a result of experiencing abuse in a relationship. There is a range of techniques and self-help ideas suggested within these pages and many of these follow the basic principles of cognitive behavioural therapy (CBT).

Cognitive behavioural therapy (CBT) is a type of approach which focuses on how your thoughts, affect your feelings and behaviour. Understanding these thoughts enables us to check out which ones are ours and which ones have been planted by our abusive partner.

The goal is for you to understand and be better able to deal with your particular circumstances. Using the methods contained in this book will empower you through the use of your own strengths, resources and coping skills and will help you to avoid repeating unhealthy and redundant patterns of behaviour.

The book uses this particular model of learning as I believe that the more you know and can understand about domestic abuse and violence and how it affects you, the better equipped you are to deal with the impact of it.

Remember you are entitled to equal respect and were in no way responsible for the abuse you received.

Self Protection

During stressful, psychologically damaging times in our lives, such as living with an abusive partner, we learn ways of coping that are based on self-protection and the minimisation of risk. Unfortunately, these methods can turn out to be less than helpful when trying to rebuild our lives and relationships once we have left.

I am going to introduce you to a key concept used throughout the book; Negative Automatic Thinking (NATs).

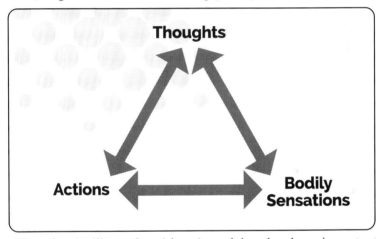

The triangle illustration (above) explains the three important areas that influence how we behave. Most of the time, we function simply by being aware of our feelings and behaviour.

However, before we become aware of a particular feeling, we will have had a very quick thought followed by a corresponding response that will generate that feeling. The behaviour that follows is a response to this feeling. Generally, we are often unaware of the original thought.

In situations where we are aware of feeling uncomfortable, stressed or frightened, it is quite probable that we will have had one of these Negative Automatic Thoughts. These NATs are instrumental in how we behave but as I have said we are often unaware of them taking place.

Over the next few weeks, we are going to try and understand these thought processes and work out ways to recognise and challenge them.

We all have NATs and some affect us more than others. For instance, I never sang as a child or as an adult. I didn't sing to my children when they were babies and I never even sang in the car alone. If someone suggested singing at a party or an evening out I would find an excuse not to take part or I would leave as the thought of it made me feel so anxious.

A colleague challenged me one day about why I didn't sing so I started to reflect on why I knew I had such a dreadful voice that it couldn't be inflicted on anyone. During this reflection, I remembered that in my first week at secondary school when I was 11 years old, I auditioned for the class choir. I remembered how the singing teacher singled me out, told me I had made a terrible noise and made me leave the class. That humiliation and shame silenced me for more than 40 years. That was one incident that had a huge impact on me.

You were probably subjected to ongoing criticism and put-downs for a long time, and learning to identify which beliefs you hold, are based on abuse from your ex-partner, starts with understanding that thinking. This chapter will help start that process.

And my own singing? My partner bought me some singing lessons for Christmas several years ago (I was not amused!). But, I went along and although I did nothing but cry during the first lesson I eventually opened my mouth and tried to make a sound.

I'm in a choir now and I attend singing workshops regularly. I sang a solo on my partner's birthday! This shows we can undo those negative thought patterns.

Negative Automatic Thoughts (NATs)

The negativity bias is the phenomena by which humans give more psychological weight to bad experiences than good ones. In fact, some researchers assert that negative emotions have an impact close to three times stronger than positive emotions. This negative bias means that we have a tendency to not only register negative stimuli more readily but also to dwell on these events. This psychological phenomenon also explains why past traumas can have such long lingering effects.

As humans, we tend to:
- Remember traumatic experiences better than positive ones.
- Recall insults better than praise.
- React more strongly to negative stimuli.
- Think about negative things more frequently than positive ones.
- Respond more strongly to negative events than to equally positive ones.

Each of us has the potential to suffer from negative thinking. It can take only a few bad things happen to us over a short period of time or for us to receive negative messages from colleagues or friends and we can have a crisis of confidence leading to our self-image taking a bit of a downward slide.

This response can mean we start to question the beliefs we hold about ourselves. We can swiftly move from thinking something like 'I'm good at my job' to 'maybe I do some of it wrong' and onwards to 'I'm lousy at my job'. It really doesn't take very long to start thinking negatively, especially if those negative thoughts are reinforced by an abusive partner telling you 'you are rubbish at your job'.

Once we have arrived at the final thought there is a tendency for us to get into a spiral of Negative Automatic Thinking which will continually reinforce our low self-esteem and poor self-belief.

These negative thinking patterns affect how we feel about ourselves. We will then begin to feel depressed and this also adds to the continual lowering of our self-esteem and confidence. This will affect how we behave in our relationships with others and the outside world. As a result, we can start to isolate ourselves, for instance, if we believe we are lousy at our job, as in the example above, we might stop going to lunch with colleagues or meeting up with them outside of work.

These negative thoughts then start to appear spontaneously and frequently. If you were in an abusive relationship for a long period of time and therefore had to cope with your self-esteem and beliefs being challenged and eroded on a daily basis, the chances are you will have developed NATS with the consequences as described.

Throughout this book, I will show you ways which can help you to overcome this way of thinking and replace it with positive thinking. This, in turn, will help improve your self-esteem and confidence and have a positive effect on the choices you make about how you live your life. Following an abusive relationship, it is likely that you will continue to experience some negative automatic thinking, and that that is ok, as by the end of the book you will have skills to deal with it more effectively.

Thought Diaries

Thoughts are not facts, they are mental events, and thus we can influence them. Our moods can also powerfully impact our thoughts.

One of the best ways to keep track of all this is to keep a *Thought Diary*. Writing a *Thought Diary* will enable you to challenge the way you think by allowing you to become more aware of the content of your own thoughts over a period of time.

You'll be able to use this simple tool to help you identify the Negative Automatic Thoughts. "Ahh, but what will that change?" I hear you say.

Well, once you know what you are thinking, you'll be able to question, challenge and alter those Negative Automatic Thoughts.

How to question and alter negative thinking

Luckily, once we've identified these ingrained Negative Automatic Thought patterns they can be dismissed. It takes a little practice but once you've learned to investigate them they no longer hold such power over your thinking and beliefs. Think of this process as a straight forward investigation, and like any investigator, it takes training and practice to spot the clues.

Firstly, what is the evidence? Do the actual facts of the situation back up the negative thoughts you are experiencing or do these facts contradict them?

Secondly, what alternative views are there to your negative thoughts? Remember, there are many different ways to look at your experiences. In what other ways could you look at what happened to you when you were in an abusive relationship?

Think of as many alternatives as you can and review the evidence for and against each of them. When you consider you experiences objectively, which alternative is most likely to be correct?

Thirdly, what is the effect of thinking the way you do? How does what you think influence how you feel or what you do? What disadvantages do you encounter when thinking the way you do? What advantages, if any, do you experience? Can you find an alternative way of thinking which will have a positive effect?

"When I first heard about Negative Automatic Thoughts (NATs) I was both surprised and relieved. I had always thought the negative thoughts were just a part of me or had become a part of me.

I couldn't really remember what my thought processes were before I met my ex-husband, the man who went on to abuse me. It never occurred to me that the negative way I processed my thoughts had a name or a description.

I felt awful to think that my behaviour was affected by these thought processes and that this could also affect others. But, I felt a willingness to learn and to change. 'I can do this' I thought.

Learning about NATs made me feel a lot better about myself, and I learned that it was perfectly natural for me to respond to the world I inhabited in this way. It comes down to the confusion I experienced whilst in the abusive relationship and the survival strategies I adopted during that time.

By the end of our first week I felt more in control, I knew what the plan was and I started to look forward to the next part of the programme. It wasn't as daunting or anxiety-inducing as I had made it out to be in my head."

JG

Thinking Errors

We will look in more detail at the thinking errors we make in a later chapter, but for now, believe me when I say you will be making them (everyone does!). You will have developed specific thinking errors as a response to the abuse you experienced as a psychological means of coping.

However, now that you have moved on from your former relationship, ask yourself if you need to think in that negative way any longer? As you continue reading I will show you some examples of the negative thought patterns you may be making and demonstrate to you that you no longer need to think in this way, especially now you have left the abusive relationship!

Remember the following:

• Negative Automatic Thoughts (NATs), as the name implies, are automatic. They just pop up without any effort on your part. These have been learned as a result of the behaviour of your abusive ex-partner.

• NATs are distorted – they don't fit the facts if you look at the hard evidence.

• NATs are always unhelpful – they keep your self-esteem low and make it difficult to change things for the better.

• NATs are plausible and believable, and because they are, it often doesn't occur to us to question them.

• NATs are involuntary, that means because they just appear without any prompting, they can be difficult to switch off.

Don't be put off

Please don't be daunted by any of this, it may seem like a lot of information to take in, but over the coming weeks, it will sink in. It may help to read these pages repeatedly in order to really understand and digest the information.

Remember, we all have these Negative Automatic Thoughts and are all influenced by them. We also spend a lot of time trying to understand them and challenging them.

It is impossible to get rid of them completely, everyone has some, and this book will not get rid of all of yours. But, the NATs that require the most attention are those that have developed as a result of the abusive relationship. In fact, when we start to identify these NATs I bet that you'll recognise the voice of your abuser in your head, after all, that's who put them there!

Exercise

This week you can start a *Thought Diary* of your own. I've included the first *Thought Diary* outline on page 30 (A modified *Thought Diary* page appears in the following chapters). You may wish to record in a notebook instead. We do recommend recording so that you can look back and see your progress.

Remember, this is for your eyes only and therefore you can write what you want in it. Start by making a daily entry simply stating how your day has been and give yourself a score out of ten for 'being myself'.

A score of one means you've been nothing like you would want to be. You may have spent the day pleasing other people, compromising what you've wanted, feeling stressed, uneasy, unhappy or doing things you didn't want to do. A score of ten means you have been able to be yourself as you wish to be.

So that's week one! Please, please, please don't be tempted to read any further. If you want to continue reading simply re-read this first week.

GOOD LUCK!

Thought Diary

Date	How have you felt today?	Rating 1 to 10
		1 = Dreadful / 10 = Really Good

WEEK TWO
The Dynamics Of Domestic Abuse

Welcome back! How did writing in your *Thought Diary* go? Did you surprise yourself and see that you had some good days being entered? Getting into the habit of recording how you feel every day is a good start. It can be surprising as we write down how we feel, both positively and negatively.

You may have been pleasantly surprised by what you scored or you may have been shocked at how low you are feeling. Identifying how you feel is the first step in helping you identify the thinking that precedes that emotion. Over the course of the book, we can then identify the unconscious thoughts that have been planted by the abusive partner. It can be useful to continue to give yourself a daily score throughout the following weeks in addition to completing the suggested exercises.

This and your *Thought Diary* will enable you to be clear about the progress you have made when we get to the end.

The Dynamics Of Intimate Partner Abuse

This week I am going to be giving you a lot of information about what is known as the 'dynamics of intimate partner abuse'. Don't be put off by that description. You will probably recognise a lot of the information contained in the following pages but some of it will not be so familiar when it comes to your own experience of living in an abusive relationship.

Within abusive relationships, there is a subtle escalation of the misuse of power and control. This chapter explains the insidious growth in control that takes place in an abusive relationship which will have resulted in you being made to feel responsible and guilty for the abuse that was directed at you. Abuse isn't always physical and this has now been recognised in law. Since 2017 it has been illegal to coercively control (emotionally abuse) someone you are in a relationship with. This includes acts of assault, threats, humiliation and intimidation or other abuse that is used to harm, punish, or frighten you.

It's Like Living With A Dictator

First of all, we are going to think about how power and control work in the larger social environment. Think about countries around the world that have dictators or very powerful regimes dominated by a handful of people.

Within these regimes, the individual with power controls everyone's lives in that country by direct and indirect means. They do this by controlling the food supplies, imports and exports, housing opportunities, what employment citizens may have and what health care they can access. They may also dictate what people wear, what religions they can practice, even who they can have relationships with. They often dictate the use of transport, immigration, jobs and education. They also monitor and control what information people have access to on television, newspapers and radio, as well as many other aspects. This allows the dictator and government to control what people understand about the world they inhabit and this, in turn, influences the population's way of thinking.

There are many examples of extreme government regimes. As an exercise let's think about how those populations living under such a regime are affected by that control. How might they behave? What will they feel? They may feel powerless, scared, intimidated, tired, suspicious, anxious, depressed, hopeless, withdrawn. How will they act? If they have never known any other way of living, they may even have an unrealistic feeling of safety.

As a result of these feelings, the populations may act secretively, lie, form sub-groups such as underground resistance movements, criminal enterprises, control of locations, these, in turn, can result in a range of behaviours that can include, acceptance, self-harm, suicide, alcohol or drug abuse, escape, collusion.

With all that in mind, where do you think the safest place might be when living under this kind of abusive regime?

It's often safest to be as close as you can to the dictator, to collude and be in favour of their regime. From this closeness, you can try and anticipate the current trends in the regime's thinking and the corresponding behaviour they will expect. This pattern of adopted or engineered behaviour would give you a significant chance of minimising the danger to yourself and any family.

That's why in all countries where you have dictators you also have those that inform or collude with the regimes. Think of Stalinist Russia, Nazi Germany, the genocide in Rwanda and more recently some of the countries affected by the 'Arab Spring'.

It's All About Power And Control

When you read the previous descriptions of dictatorial social control did you recognise anything? It's very likely that you will have noticed similarities between living under a dictatorship and living with your former abusive intimate partner.

Your abuser will have controlled many aspects if not every aspect of the world you were living in. They may have made all the big decisions about where you lived; they may have prevented you from having a job or only allowed you to do certain types of work.

Your abusive partner may have dictated what food was eaten in the household and how much was spent on fuel and phone bills. They would probably have chosen what was watched on television, what films were seen, what papers and books were read. They could have chosen the social occasions you attended and who you interacted with. They may have dictated when you had sex and how and even when you conceived and how many children you had.

Some of you may have watched the film *Sleeping with the Enemy* (1991) starring Julia Roberts or read the book it is based on by Nancy Price. (if you decide to watch the film or read the book please be mindful that you may find it upsetting or even re-traumatising.). In the early part of the story, Julia Roberts' character Laura Burney is attending a social function with her husband, Martin Burney (played by Patrick Bergin) and he not only chooses what she should wear but once at the party he controls who she is talking to with a single glance.

All the patterns of behaviour and feelings I describe above in relation to how people survive under a dictatorship would have been the same as or similar to the many strategies you adopted in order to cope with living as you were.

Hence my referring to them as coping strategies. In the same way that they would be absolutely necessary for you to stay safe living under a dictatorial regime, they were the only way to manage the risks you were experiencing living in an abuser's regime.

Now as you have left that regime of abuse, the issue is that if you continue to use these same coping strategies, they may prevent you from truly moving forward with your life. There were very good reasons to be secretive and possibly lie to your former partner when you were in an abusive intimate relationship, but if you continue with these strategies they can stop you from forming new relationships with friends and/or new partners.

A Question Of Trust

It may be difficult to trust others after what you have been through. Being scared, frightened, anxious, depressed and/or suicidal are all responses we subconsciously or deliberately adopt as a reaction to the awfulness of our situation.

The suspicion we adopt in order to deal with our abusive intimate relationship is a totally understandable method of protecting ourselves, especially when you take into account that the one person we rightly expect to be able to trust, our partner, lets us down and hurts us again and again. Unfortunately, to continue to be suspicious and untrusting will more than likely prevent us from forming healthy relationships moving forwards.

Addiction And Overuse

If using alcohol or drugs was part of how you survived or you were encouraged to use or become addicted to substances by your abusive partner as a way of them controlling you, then this too needs to be addressed.

Remember

You are not to blame. All these behaviours were coping strategies used to keep you and any family members safe. It may be that you will need specialist help for these issues and on page 148 I have listed contact numbers for organisations that can help you access support.

34

Cognitive Dissonance

The situations you dealt with when you were with your abuser gave rise to many necessary patterns of responsive behaviour including suspicion and submission. So what was it that happened to your thinking when you were dealing with that relationship, with all the contradictions you encountered?

In psychological terms being in a situation where we have two sets of contradictory thoughts at the same time, puts the individual in a situation that psychologists call 'cognitive dissonance'.

Cognitive dissonance refers to the mental conflict that occurs when a person's behaviours and beliefs do not align. It may also happen when a person holds two beliefs that contradict one another. Cognitive dissonance causes feelings of unease and tension, and people attempt to relieve this discomfort in different ways. Examples include "explaining things away" or rejecting new information that conflicts with their existing beliefs.

As people generally have an innate desire to avoid this discomfort, cognitive dissonance has a significant effect on a person's behaviours, thoughts, decisions, beliefs and attitudes and mental health.

People experiencing cognitive dissonance may notice that they feel anxious, guilty and/or ashamed. As a result, they may try to hide their actions or beliefs from others or rationalise their actions or choices continuously. They can also shy away from conversations or debates about specific topics in order to avoid learning new information that goes against their existing beliefs.

Avoiding factual information can allow people to continue maintaining behaviours with which they do not fully agree. Situations where cognitive dissonance can occur include:

- Smoking despite being aware of the adverse health effects of tobacco use.
- Choosing to promote a behaviour, such as regular exercise, that a person does not themselves practice.
- Telling a lie despite the person thinking of themselves as honest.
- Purchasing a new car that is not fuel efficient, despite being environmentally conscious.
- Eating meat while also thinking of themselves as an animal lover who dislikes the thought of killing animals.

35

Individuals may persuade themselves that no conflict exists. Alternatively, a person may find a way to justify behaviours that conflict with their beliefs. It involves a person changing their behaviours so that they are consistent with their other beliefs.

For example: 'My partner loves me, my partner hurts me'. These two statements would appear to contradict the expected pattern of behaviour. We all experience contradictory thoughts but used by an abuser it is also a way of brainwashing.

Seen together, the words cognitive and dissonance may sound complicated. To put it simply, cognitive dissonance, when applied to an abusive relationship, refers to the contradictory thoughts and behaviour like those mentioned above.

We know that cults intentionally put potential members into the psychological position of cognitive dissonance to control them and convert them! The process the target undergoes is unconscious and they will not have been aware of the changes they were making in their thinking and neither will you.

How It Works

You are in a situation that is uncomfortable because it is either unsatisfactory or feels scary. You have two different views or thoughts about the situation. This can lead to confusion or anxiety.

For example: I'll assume that when you first began the relationship that turned abusive, you would have considered yourself an assertive person, but this will have changed thanks to the behaviour of your abuser.

Over time your abusive partner may have started to demand that their evening meal was cooked by you and ready on the table for them at 6pm, when they get home from work. This was difficult for you as you also worked and only got home shortly before the time they'd set. You still tried to get the food on the table on time. But it was not always possible. At first, your partner was disappointed, but the situation continued and escalated. Your partner became more aggressive and at one point they threw the food you'd prepared at you when it was late to the table.

This situation made you anxious and frightened and unconsciously your thoughts and your behaviour changed. Now tea was always ready at the time set by your abusive partner and you started to justify the change in your own behaviour.

In order to cope you justified it by changing the conflicting thoughts to ones that seemed reasonable but were in fact, you changing your behaviour to meet the demands of your partner.

For example: "Having tea ready at a set time isn't a problem for me". You were putting their needs above your own. This is followed by thoughts along the lines of "my partner has every right to expect tea at a certain time, they are the breadwinner".

However, in adopting this pattern of thinking you will have had to let go of any belief that you are assertive. So in this way, something fundamental about the way you think about yourself has changed and this will have affected your beliefs and the way you see the world.

Thanks to cognitive dissonance, this capitulation also changes the positive beliefs we have about ourselves and turns them into negative beliefs. It is well-known that when we are children, parenting that is 'good enough', enables us to develop positive mental health and grow into independent, confident and trusting individuals. Being in an abusive intimate relationship reverses that positive mental health and corresponding patterns of behaviour.

It's Important To Remember

Positive mental health enables the following:

- We feel in control of our own life and destiny. As children, we learn to make decisions based on evidence and in a healthy relationship with our parents we are encouraged to practice this.
- We find we are able to form positive relationships because we have been supported in developing relationships and learning how to set appropriate boundaries to protect ourselves.
- We feel good about ourselves as we have been given positive feedback and been told we are a good person.
- We are in touch with feelings because we have been taught about the range of feelings people have and how to manage difficult feelings as well as positive ones.
- We know how to look after ourselves as we have been taught self-care skills by our parents.
- We are able to make rational decisions as again we have been taught about actions and consequences by our parents.

All of this positive parenting installs positive inner beliefs which, while we may be unconscious of them, influence all aspects of our daily life.

As you will have noticed I like to use comparisons, such as that of someone in an abusive relationship being compared to someone who is living under a dictatorial regime. I use these comparisons to illustrate the fact that what you have been through and the control you have sacrificed is every bit as important and all-encompassing as those who have lived under strict dictatorial control.

Another comparison illustrates why individuals will remain in an abusive relationship for many years before leaving their abuser. You may have heard of Stockholm Syndrome. The term is often used to describe how a victim may come to support those victimising them. This term can be applied to those being abused in intimate relationships.

What Is Stockholm Syndrome?

The term Stockholm Syndrome is the name given to a condition which causes a hostage to develop a psychological bond with their captor. It stems from an incident at a bank in Stockholm, Sweden, in 1973, when two gunmen robbing the bank held four people hostage for several days during a siege in which the police surrounded the building.

During the siege and despite the gunmen making threats, the captives relationship with their captors changed dramatically. This change, brought about by the captors' psychological games, resulted in the hostages showing sympathy for the gunmen after their release. One hostage even became engaged to one of her captors.[1]

Is An Abusive Relationship Really Like That?

Yes, it is! Think about some of the ways in which you felt towards your abusive ex-partner.

- You probably had some positive feelings towards them.
- You may have had negative feelings towards your family or friends, especially if you felt they were trying to rescue you from the relationship. The same goes for anyone from the authorities.
- You may have supported your abuser's reasoning and behaviours.

38

- You may have undertaken supportive behaviours to help your abuser.
- It could be the case that your responses to the abuse may have unintentionally stifled the chance that would have seen you removed from the abusive relationship.

But, Why Would I Risk This?

There are several conditions that serve as a foundation for the development of Stockholm syndrome within an abusive relationship. These are the same conditions that are found in many hostage situations.

- The existence of a perceived threat to your survival, either psychological or physical, along with the belief that the person employing the threat will carry it out
- The belief that for you escape is impossible
- The existence of a perceived small kindness from the abuser to the victim
- Isolation from other perspectives than your own and your abusers

Don't Forget There's Also Cognitive Dissonance.

When we have two sets of cognitions (knowledge, opinion, feelings) that are opposite, our own and our abuser's, and the situation becomes emotionally uncomfortable.

When your partner becomes abusive, and you can't leave for a variety of reasons, through cognitive dissonance you begin to tell yourself:
- They only do it because they are stressed.
- They only hit me sometimes.
- It's not their fault.

Sometimes it is easier to believe these excuses than to accept that the person we love is hurting us. Abusive partners make us feel that it is us who is responsible for the abuse, that somehow we are the guilty party. It is very important to remind yourself that the responsibility for the abuse and resulting behaviours belongs with the abuser.

"I found it hard to explore what domestic abuse meant because I thought that domestic abuse only referred to the physical violence within a relationship. I was very confused with trying to come to terms with the reality of what had happened to me. A part of me was still in denial as I felt most aspects of the abusive relationship I was in were my fault.

I read through the descriptions of what constituted abuse and coercion and I felt sick. It was then I acknowledged that what I had gone through was abuse and there hadn't been anything I could've done to change my abuser's behaviour.

At first, it was hard to take all this in as I was several months out of the relationship before I learned that what I had been going through had a name. Coercive Control isn't easy to digest. I was ticking off each of the symptoms and the comparisons to the struggle faced by prisoners of war, but I wondered how could my experience compare to something so horrific and terrifying as that experienced by a prisoner of war? I thought that it was a bit extreme to compare the two but I soon realised that was being described was what I had suffered from for years.

I realised that I was being nice to think that my abuser was just a 24/7 bully. I learned his behaviour was much more than that, it was intentional and harmful. I thought I was protecting myself by originally thinking his behaviour was due to his past and his poor self-esteem.

The descriptions of an abuser's behaviour (in a POW camp) to the behaviour of my own abuser that hurt me the most; deprivation of toilet, sleeping on the floor, pregnancy etc. Was it all really planned? I had spent the last months, before my discovery, pitying him but now I felt bitter and angry about the whole set-up.

While I was going through the family court system I was still having to see my ex-husband each weekend to hand over the kids for his allowed access time. I felt like I was still in the relationship as he continued to play the same games in his attempt to regain control.

Hearing about Stockholm Syndrome and how being in an abusive relationship was similar to how a hostage can develop a relationship with their kidnapper taught me that for those in an abusive relationship it wasn't as simple as running away and cutting ties.

I believed my abuser's threats, despite him not always carrying them out. I didn't believe I could escape as I had tried a few times

> *before and had always gone back. On one occasion I was away*
> *from him for just under two weeks and I was living in my mum's*
> *small flat with her partner. During that time I never felt so alone.*
> *I sat in the flat with my children losing the will to stay away from*
> *him. I wanted him to declare he was going to change for the better,*
> *so I could be released from my fears and go home. I had become*
> *dependent on him."*
>
> **JG**

Another eye-opening comparison is that made between those who have suffered physical and mental abuse in an intimate relationship and those who have suffered psychological torture, brainwashing and physical torture during wartime.

Biderman's Cycle of Coercive Control,[2] which was originally designed to describe the feelings of those who had lived in prisoner of war camps and experienced torture during the Korean War (1950 to 1953) can be applied to the experience of domestic abuse.

With Prisoners of War (POWs), the first stage is isolation by keeping them in solitary confinement. The second stage is exhaustion by keeping the lights on to stop them sleeping. The third stage is through the use of humiliation. Strip them, make them use the toilet in full view, and fourth make threats to kill them or their family.

If you look at the Biderman's Cycle applied to domestic abuse you will see that the development of the abusive relationship was not a random or unintentional pattern of behaviour on the part of your abuser. Rather, it was an effective way of undermining you and controlling you. I have also included a list of comparisons between POWs and those who live with domestic violence.

Following your escape from the abusive relationship you may have figured this out, but if not, this may be a revelation for you. Hopefully, it is also another piece of information that reinforces the fact that you were not responsible for the abuse you suffered. When you were unable to leave the relationship, you were not being compliant with the abuse or responsible for it.

41

Exercises

As I mentioned earlier, much of the programme outlined in this book is based on the principles of Cognitive Behaviour Therapy and as such the intention is to encourage you to reflect on ways to support yourself as you move away from the coping strategies that served you during the time of abuse, but that are now no longer of any use.

With this in mind I have suggested a few 'nice' things to do for your homework. You can either choose one on the list and try to do it three times during the week, or you can choose three different ideas and do them once each. Sometimes we can find it hard to do nice things for ourselves because we have been led to believe that we don't deserve it so this can take practice.

Record what your thoughts were about carrying out the activity and how you felt doing it. Record any interruptions that take place during your activities and how you felt being interrupted. Also, jot down how you felt after you'd finished the activity. Of course, you may want to think up your own activity but make it fairly simple and pleasant.

Suggestions:

• Bathe with candles and stay in the bath for at least half an hour.
• Go for a walk on your own.
• Watch a video.
• Paint your fingers or toenails.
• Plant some bulbs.

What makes you stressed?

What situations make you feel stressed?	
How do you deal with the stressful situations you encounter?	
Which of the techniques in this book do you think will help you deal with stress?	
How might the techniques listed in the book make you feel better?	
Do you use any exercises to lower your levels of stress? If so, which ones?	

Biderman's Cycle Of Coercion

Isolation

I want to spend more time with you
You're the most important thing
Family tension - turning around situations
Calls/texts/emails - I love/miss you
I'll pick you up
Turning up
Interrupting hobbies – let's do something together
Ingratiating to family
I'm shy/insecure/not good enough
Moving of bank account, GP
Moving in together
No need for two cars
Joint tenancy
Discourage friends/test loyalties
'Be with me' (normal love)
Flattery, you're special etc
Checking up, going everywhere with you
Comments on family
Emotional blackmail

Exhaustion

Responsibility for happiness falls on you alone
Their needs dominate
Sexual demands
Pregnancy
Loss of sleep/sleep deprivation
Housework – to excess
Constant criticism
Comparisons to others
Jealousy
Child care
Guilt
Unpredictably/moving goalposts
Mood swings
Absence from work excuses
Dependency on alcohol/drugs
Illness
Depression/medication
Anxiety/shame
Losing of identity
Hiding/lying to others

Biderman's Cycle Of Coercion

Degradation

Dehumanisation
Rejection of food offered
Infidelity
Eat off the floor/sleep on the floor
Permission to do basic things
Deprivation of toilet/sanitary wear
Withholding of sex/affection
Flaunting sex with others
Withholding of money
Sexual acts eg three in a bed, prostitution,
bondage, filming, anal sex, animals, rape
Pornography, watching it, making it
Children threats/abuse
Drugs/drink

Threats

If you leave, I'll find you
I'll kill you/I'll kill myself
I'll kill the children
No one will believe you
You are mad etc/get you sectioned
Can't manage without me
No one else will want you
No one to go to/no friends
I'll beat up x, y or z
Silent treatment
Particular look
I'll scar you
Property damage
Attack pets
Take children away
Social services
Withholding money, medication, drugs

Biderman's Cycle Of Coercion

Prisoner of War	Someone living with domestic abuse/violence
Physically imprisoned – cannot leave unless released by guards	May be able to leave if abuser doesn't physically imprison them
Not alone and not isolated – they are with their peers who are in the same situation	Physically and emotionally isolated from friends and family
Abuse ends when war ends – captors will not try to find them after it ends	There may not be an end – abuser likely to find them and further abuse if they leave
Given support by family, friends and society whatever their behaviour towards their captors	Little sympathy from friends, family and agencies who may judge them e.g. because they are seen to have provoked or because they haven't left
Return to a safe home after the war ends, with family and friends	Already at home – for the abuse to end they may have to leave their home, often with nothing, losing everything

Thought Diary

Date	Situation	Emotions	Automatic Thought	Challenges?
		What were you feeling?	The first thought you had?	Is there a challenge to the thought?

47

WEEK THREE
Self-Esteem

H ow did your exercise go? What did you decide to do? Did you follow the suggestions listed in the previous chapter? Hopefully, you've written down what you decided to do and how you felt during that time. Taking note of how you felt and your response to those feelings, did you find it hard to do something just for you?

Many individuals I've worked with tell me that this exercise is really hard. They have spent so long being told they are selfish and worthless and don't deserve anything nice or that if they take time for themselves they are accused of not caring or loving the abusive person, that they have just stopped doing anything for themselves. So, if you found this difficult just think about whose voice was in your head? If it was your ex-partner just revisit the information on Negative Automatic Thoughts (NATs) on page 24, and in this chapter see if you can link the thoughts you've had to a NAT.

One participant I worked with chose as her activity having a bath with a bath bomb and candles! She lived on her own with no children or anyone to care for so there was no reason why she couldn't do this. However, when describing what had happened her diary entries showed the following:

- Emotion - she felt anxious.
- Automatic thought - I shouldn't be doing this I'm lazy.
- Evidence for this - None. But this is where it suddenly dawned on her that this was the result of her abuser telling her she was lazy for more than 20 years. Having recognised this her challenge now was to accept that she was not lazy and that she

had every right to take her bath. I hope you also have some of these lightbulb moments.

Human Rights

You will probably have heard of the term 'Human Rights'. This term is often heard being talked about on the TV or Radio in reference to those populations living under dictatorship or those living in developing countries, with larger poor populations. The United Nations describes them as follows:

"Human rights are rights inherent to all human beings, regardless of race, sex, nationality, ethnicity, language, religion, or any other status. Human rights include the right to life and liberty, freedom from slavery and torture, freedom of opinion and expression, the right to work and education, and many more. Everyone is entitled to these rights, without discrimination." [1]

A Bill Of Rights

It is widely acknowledged that these rights belong to everyone and despite what you may think, that includes you. Reading through the fairly long list of rights that appear on page 50, it might shock you to know that you are as entitled as the next person to every one of them. It may be some time since you were aware you had any rights, let alone were in a position exercise them.

Complementing the Bill of Rights checklist is the Responsibility checklist (page 51). The combination of the two will give you an idea of how you are entitled to be treated and what responsibilities you have towards yourself. Neither list is exhaustive but they will help you to acknowledge that every aspect of you as an individual is important. You count for something and you matter. Your feelings can be trusted and the way you think is also appropriate. You have the right to value your wants and needs. You're not here to serve anyone and you have the right to object to any abuse or constant mistreatment.

Remind yourself: "I have rights and it is my responsibility to assert these rights. The decisions I make and the way I conduct myself will reflect my self-esteem." [2]

An Introduction To Self-Esteem

Self-esteem is closely linked to any belief system we adopt about ourselves. Healthy self-esteem equates with feeling good, whereas low self-esteem equates with our feeling bad. If you have lived with domestic abuse you may have spent years having your belief systems undermined and eroded by constant criticism, belittling and psychological abuse.

As a result of this constant conditioning, you may well have internalised the abuser's perspective of you. This will have altered the core beliefs you once held about yourself.

Remember, this change was not your fault, but an unconscious and necessary psychological mechanism for keeping you safe and coping with the cognitive dissonance you experienced. No matter how high your self-esteem was at the beginning of the relationship or how long-standing your positive core belief systems were, no individual can sustain a positive self-image against a consistent regime of psychological abuse.

The negative and pejorative criticism that you have been bombarded with by your intimate abuser will have resulted in your replacing your previously positive self-image with your abuser's negative image. This negative image will have resulted in your developing Negative Automatic Thoughts that will have reinforced your low self-esteem and negative core beliefs day in, day out.

For some of you, it might be difficult to relate to ever having had any positive core beliefs. You may have experienced abuse as a child and, where your parent(s) weren't able to provide you with good enough parenting or were directly abusive, you may have developed negative core beliefs from an early age. While these may make some of the self-help exercises contained in this book more difficult for you, attempting them will still have a positive impact if you are able to persevere.

What happened to you was not your fault, your rights were undermined, and your abuser didn't allow you to be responsible for yourself. Now that you have left the abusive relationship you have the opportunity to choose your beliefs about yourself and practice reinforcing them.

I am not going to pretend that this is easy for everyone so the trick is to read, understand, do the exercises and practice, practice, practice!

We've already taken a quick look at what Negative Automatic Thoughts (NATs) are. Below is a list of what they can and can't do and why they offer nothing of value to your new life:

1. They are not based on evidence - when we pick them apart and try and find any truth to them there isn't any. Despite that lack of evidence they still feel believable, especially when our self- esteem is low. When you begin to record your negative thoughts it's best to start thinking about those that affect your behaviour (e.g. when you start avoiding people because you think they won't like you), rather than those NATs you have about you as a person (e.g. I'm difficult). The fact is that both of these negative thoughts will have been planted and reinforced by your abuser, but it will probably be easier for you to challenge those NATs that concern your behaviour towards others to start with.

2. They are predictive - This means they appear to say something about the future. This is, of course, impossible to know - e.g. you think something along the lines of "If I go to the party I will make a fool of myself?" There is no evidence for this. Remember, neither NATs nor your former abuser can predict the future.

3. They are based on your abuser's perspective – This will be something they have told you about yourself. For example: "You always iron the clothes wrong?".

4. Remember to survive your abuse you were forced to see everything from your intimate abusers perspective. With that in mind, it's not too difficult to see how this then translates into you taking on their perspective at an unconscious level.

YOUR BILL OF RIGHTS

- I have the right to be safe.
- I have the right to say NO.
- I have the right to make mistakes.
- I have the right to be me.
- I have the right to love and be loved.

- I have the right to be treated with respect.
- I have the right to be human – NOT PERFECT.
- I have the right to make decisions about anything that affects me.
- I have the right to put myself first.
- I have the right to be angry and protest if I am being treated unfairly or abusively by anyone.
- I have the right to my own privacy.
- I have the right to my own opinions, to express them and to be taken seriously.
- I have the right to earn and control my own money.
- I have the right to change my mind.
- I have the right not to be responsible for other adults' problems.
- I have the right not to be liked by everyone.
- I have the right to control my own life and to change it if I am not happy with it.

I AM RESPONSIBLE

- I am responsible for myself.
- I am responsible for tending to my spiritual, emotional, physical and financial wellbeing.
- I am responsible for identifying and meeting my needs.
- I am responsible for solving my problems or learning to live with those I cannot solve.
- I am responsible for my choices.
- I am responsible for what I give and receive.
- I am responsible for setting and achieving my goals.
- I am responsible for how much I enjoy my life.
- I am responsible for whom I love and how I choose to express this love.
- I am responsible for my wants and desires.

Self-care is not selfish, as some people might assume it is. It is the responsibility you have to your own wellbeing.

On the following page, I have included a Self-Esteem Checklist.[3] Take a good look at it and be honest with yourself. Take your time and think about what you believe to be true about yourself?

The Self-Esteem Checklist

What do you believe to be true about yourself?
Look at the following list and put the words 'I am' in front of each one. *Why not rate yourself?*
Score 0 for almost never. Score 1 for sometimes.
Score 2 for Often. Score 3 for almost always.

_____ Tolerant	_____ Capable	_____ Stupid
_____ Interesting	_____ Guilty	_____ Adventurous
_____ Lovable	_____ Optimistic	_____ Sensitive
_____ Kind	_____ Reflective	_____ Self-aware
_____ Trustworthy	_____ Amusing	_____ Happy
_____ Intelligent	_____ Rigid	_____ Proud
_____ Unemotional	_____ Self-conscious	_____ Miserable
_____ Controlled	_____ Controlling	_____ Irritable
_____ Demanding	_____ Bossy	_____ Angry
_____ Free	_____ Nice	_____ Lazy
_____ Boring	_____ Passive	_____ Foolish

Thinking Points

Look at where you scored yourself as a 3

These are descriptions you believe you're 'almost always'?
These characteristics are part of your self-image. Are they
positive or negative? How do these aspects affect your
self-esteem? Which would you like to change?

Look at where you scored 0

These descriptions are what you believe you're 'almost never'?
Your self-image does not include any of these features,
how does this affect your self-esteem? Are they positive or
negative? Would you like to increase any of these?

Which if any of the 'almost never' characteristics would you like to increase?

Use your *Thought Diary*

More About Negative Automatic Thinking

As you've already read, Negative Automatic Thoughts (NATs) are a result of low self-esteem and this developed as a result of the abuse you experienced. Remember, negative thoughts have several characteristics. Those NATs listed below explain how these distorted thinking patterns work. This will help you to fill in your *Thought Diary*.

• NATs are automatic – they pop up with no effort on your part.
• NATs are distorted – they do not fit the facts.
• NATs are unhelpful – they lower your self-esteem and make it hard to change.
• NATs often come across as perfectly plausible – it doesn't occur to us to question them.
• NATs are involuntary – they can be difficult to switch off.

It is true that the lower your self-esteem, the more negative your thoughts are likely to be. They are also more believable. Using your *Thought Diary* to keep a record of those negative thoughts will help you recognise the circumstances in which you are having them. Referencing these moments will help you to reframe them and change them for the better.

There are ten patterns of thinking that are common to Negative Automatic Thoughts. Check out the list below and see if you recognise any of the thought patterns listed.[4]

1. All Or Nothing

Everything is seen in black and white terms with no shades of grey; For example, if you don't do something perfectly you see yourself as a total failure. It is also easy to see how this NAT could have started with the abusive relationship when there could have been serious consequences if the perpetrator's rules were not followed to the letter.

2. Over Generalisation

One negative thing that occurs to you is seen as a pointer to all the things you do. For example, you may often use the words 'always' and 'never'. You make a mistake and say "I never get it right'. This is also NAT developing with the internalised voice of the perpetrator, 'you never get it right' etc.

3. Mental Filter

You let your mind focus on only the negative things and ignore the positive ones; this reinforces the belief that life seems to be a series of depressing events. This may have been to anticipate the worst things about the relationship so when it wasn't as bad as it could be it was a good day.

4. Disqualifying The Positive

This is similar to the mental filter above, although here you notice a positive event but then undermine it by saying, "anyone can do that" or "it was a lucky guess". This dismissal of the positive allows you to maintain your negative beliefs despite there being evidence to the contrary.

5. Jumping To Conclusions

You make assumptions with no evidence to support them. Perhaps someone may not notice you in the street, and you assume they have fallen out with you or are angry with you, without checking this out; or you may predict a negative outcome for something you plan to do, even though you have no evidence for this. This can be a reflection of your low self-esteem.

6. Magnification Or Minimisation

Perhaps you make mountains out of molehills or reduce the importance of positive information. Because you are late your friend will be angry with you and never want to see you again, or someone says you are interesting and a good friend and you dismiss that by saying that they probably say that to everybody and that they are only saying it to make you feel good. This can be because of your low self -esteem you don't believe you have value.

7. Emotional Reasoning

You feel it therefore it must be true, you let your heart rule your head. For example, because you feel guilty, you must have done something wrong. This can be due to the negativity and blame you constantly heard from your abuser.

8. Should Have, Ought Too And Must Do

When you tell yourself you ought or must do something and then fail or cannot do what you set out to, you criticise yourself. You leave no room for manoeuvre nor do you allow for external factors interfering. Again, this would be an attempt to stay safe by always sticking to the perpetrators perspective.

9. Labelling And Mislabelling

This is an extreme form of over-generalisation. You give yourself a label associated with the negative behaviour such as if you make a mistake, you describe yourself as hopeless. It is the event that goes wrong, but you label yourself, not the event. This would have been learnt from the perpetrator who would have been labelling you.

10. Personalisation

You assume responsibility for everything that goes wrong even when there is no evidence for it. If the washing machine breaks down, you blame yourself for mistreating it even though there is no evidence for this. In reality, blame is only reasonable if you intend something, otherwise, it is unfortunate and regrettable.

Feeling you were responsible may have given you a false sense of control and the perpetrator always blamed you anyway, feeling responsible gave you a sense that you could make it better.

Exercise

Using your *Thought Diary*, record any times you feel anxious or upset and what you were doing at the time. Thinking about all that has been said in this and previous chapters will help you to recognise your rights and reinforce your responsibilities to yourself. Understanding and keeping these diaries may be hard at first, that is a common experience, and it may take several weeks to begin to benefit from them.

Also, fill in the worksheet on page 58 and using the negative/positive lists on page 56 think about your answers carefully and remember, be honest with yourself.

List of Negative and Positive Beliefs
Responsibility - I am something 'wrong'

I don't deserve love	I deserve love; I can have love
I am a bad person	I am a good (loving) person
I am terrible	I am fine as I am
I am worthless/inadequate	I am worthy/worthwhile
I am shameful	I am honourable
I am not lovable	I am lovable
I am not good enough	I am deserving (fine/okay)
I deserve only bad things	I deserve good things
I am ugly/my body is hateful	I am fine as I am
I do not deserve...	I deserve and I can have
I am stupid/not smart enough	I am intelligent/able to learn
I am insignificant/unimportant	I am significant/important
I am a disappointment	I am good enough the way I am
I deserve to die	I deserve to live my life
I deserve to be miserable	I deserve to be happy
I am different/don't belong	I am OK as I am

Responsibility - I did something 'wrong'

I should have done something	I did the best I could
I did something wrong	I learned (can learn) from it
I should have known better	I do the best I can (I can learn)

Negative Beliefs   Positive Beliefs
Safety/Vulnerability

Negative Beliefs	Positive Beliefs
I am untrustworthy	I am trustworthy
I cannot trust myself	I can (learn to) trust myself
I cannot trust my judgement	I can trust my judgement
I cannot trust anyone	I can choose whom to trust
I cannot protect myself	I can (learn to) take care of myself
I am in danger	It's over. I am safe now
It's not ok to feel/show emotions	I can safely feel/show emotions
I cannot stand up for myself	I can make my needs known
I cannot let it out	I can choose to let it out

Control/Choice

Negative Beliefs	Positive Beliefs
I am not in control	I am now in control
I am powerless (helpless)	I now have choices
I am weak	I am strong
I cannot get what I want	I can get what I want
I am a failure (will fail)	I am not a failure
I cannot succeed	I can succeed
I must be perfect/please everyone	I can be myself/make mistakes
I cannot stand it	I can handle it
I am inadequate	I am capable
I cannot trust anyone	I can choose whom to trust

How confident are you?

Describe a situation when you felt confident. How did you behave in this situation?	
Think of a situation where you lacked confidence. How did you act in this situation?	
Give an example of how you lack confidence	
How does your behaviour influence how you are seen by others?	
What techniques do you think might help you increase your confidence?	

Thought Diary

Date	Situation	Emotions	Automatic Thought	Challenges?
		What were you feeling?	The first thought you had?	Is there a challenge to the thought?

"The self-esteem checklist was something I originally filled out without too much thought. I didn't want to over analyse how I felt and feel upset about my responses. One thing I have recognised is that the suggested actions in this book are not simplistic easy fixes.

It is true that taking the necessary time to follow them has allowed my self-esteem to change for the better. I completed the checklist again a couple of years after my first go and the difference clearly shows that continuing to work on my self-development has had a positive impact on me as a person.

Revisiting the process of discovering my Negative Automatic Thoughts a second time helped me recognise my low self-esteem and that I still needed to work on my thought processes. I was someone who always saw the bad in someone or feared the worst in everything.

My anxiety was so high at the time that I couldn't control my thought processes. Anyone who gave me a compliment would hear me picking out the bad things they supposedly hadn't seen.

I was starting to realise the habits my abusive ex-husband had created in me. His controlling behaviour had changed the blueprints of everything that made me, me. My thoughts, actions and feelings were all under his control. Thanks to the programme I learned how my responses and corresponding behaviour had a negative effect on others."

JG

WEEK FOUR
How We Cope Emotionally

Did you record any times you felt anxious or upset during the last few days? If you did, what were you doing at the time? It's a great tool that can be referred to repeatedly. Are you still keeping a daily score of how you feel?

Don't forget that what you write down in the first place may be valid at the time of writing. As you progress you will probably find your patterns of thought changing and you'll want to change the entries in your *Thought Diary*. It is best to leave them alone and to add your new thoughts. This will give you a great picture of your progress as you work your way through the book.

The Psychological Consequences Of Coping

Living with abuse and violence is exhausting, isolating, humiliating and degrading and, as for any individual living in such intolerable situations, you will have found whatever means you could in order to cope with the inflicted mental and physical pain.

As a result, it is the case that sometimes those who are living with abusive partners go on to develop difficulties with their mental health. It is also possible for some people to live in a relationship that is abusive without it having a major impact on their psychological well-being.

The degree to which you are affected will be dependent on several factors, such as the extent and length of time the abuse went on, whether or not you had support from friends or family, whether or not you were already vulnerable due to previous episodes of distress in your life.

I have worked with people who have developed depression, anxiety, obsessive-compulsive disorder and a range of other presentations of psychological distress. Some of those I have worked with have used alcohol or drugs to mask their distress and fear. In some situations, I have known abusers to encourage the use of drink and drugs as a way of further abusing people. The abuser may also issue threats such as "If you leave me, I will tell social services you take drugs and they will take the children away".

My aim is to give you an opportunity to look at the psychological mechanisms you've used in order to cope with the abuse and/or violence you encountered. I'm also aiming for you to explore, understand and respect your reasons for adopting those particular coping strategies and techniques. This week will help you to understand that any mental health difficulties you may have are likely to be a result of the abuse you endured rather than a pre-existing condition.

All abuse by an intimate partner can cause problems with the abused person's mental health in addition to their physical health. Domestic violence in female psychiatric patients is much more common than in other patient groups.

According to statistics gathered from those attending non-emergency psychiatric clinics, 60% of female patients had suffered physical domestic violence at some point in their lives. [1]

A very high proportion suffered from physical injuries but only half sought medical attention. Of those who were victims, 27% had experienced domestic violence during pregnancy. [2]

The Potential Psychological And Emotional Effects

Survivors of domestic abuse, like those that have survived a war or some other traumatic event in their lives, can suffer from psychological and/or emotional effects such as those listed below:

Alcoholism, Drug-Taking And Tobacco Misuse (Self-Medication)

It could be the case that you have used illicit substances eg cocaine, cannabis or opiates such as heroin. Perhaps you've used legal medication to aid with your situation including prescribed medications like Temazepam, Diazepam or Prozac. There are also many over the counter drugs such as Nytol, Piriton or Benylin. Perhaps one of the most common is alcohol.

Depression And Anxiety

These manifest in a variety of ways. You could find you are suffering from a lack of energy and that you feel tired all the time. Perhaps your sleep pattern is disturbed or you have no appetite.

With depression, it is not unusual to have low self-esteem, mood swings and you may also experience guilt. For some people with depression, they experience a feeling of hopelessness about the future and as a result, they can suffer suicidal thoughts.

On the other hand, you may be anxious about your health, work and family. Anxiety can bring on physical problems such as panic attacks, palpitations, nausea, sweating or dizziness.

It can also have a negative effect on you psychologically with your experiencing such things as a fear of death, a sense of unreality or fear of 'going mad'. Perhaps you're suffering from a lack of libido or fear of intercourse. Depression and anxiety manifest in many ways including those listed below.

- Eating and sleep disorders.
- Feelings of guilt and shame.
- Phobias and panic disorders.
- Poor self-esteem.
- Psychosomatic disorders – some physical diseases are thought to be affected by stress and anxiety.
- Unsafe sexual behaviour – risking STDs including HIV.
- Suicide and self-harm.

Self-Harm

Some of those who have undergone unhealthy relationships as a result of being abused by their intimate partner may develop a pattern of deliberate non-suicidal behaviour to inflict pain on themselves and this is aimed at relieving emotional stress.

These actions could take the form of cutting, burning, overdosing on prescribed medication. Hair pulling, hitting themselves and breaking bones are actions used by those in deep distress.

Post Traumatic Stress

This comes about as a result of exposure to a traumatic event or events. The person suffering from PTSD may well have experienced something traumatic. So traumatic that when they recall the experience or experience something similar they become distressed. This can be in their waking hours or dreaming when they are asleep. They commonly experience intense fear, helplessness or horror.

Complex Post Traumatic Stress

Complex Post-traumatic Stress Disorder is the result of multiple traumatic events occurring over a period of time, often referred to as 'Complex Trauma'. These can include incidents of child abuse, prolonged domestic violence, torture or slavery.

Individuals with CPTSD will experience the same core symptoms as PTSD but may also experience severe and pervasive problems in regulating feelings and emotions, deep and persistent feelings of shame, guilt or failure and difficulties in sustaining relationships and in feeling close to others. This is probably one of the most common results of domestic abuse.

Unfortunately, this is often not recognised as such and all too often an individual can spend a lot of time being misdiagnosed with a 'borderline personality disorder' suggesting it is something within the individual that is wrong rather than the situation they have been in that has resulted in the emotions and behaviours.

What Happens With Stress And Anxiety

When you experience stress your body and mind's 'flight or fight' mechanism kicks into action almost instantly. This reaction prepares us to cope with perceived threats. Our remarkable bodies use every available means to overcome our fears and deal with the stressful situation.

This is where dramatic hormonal, physical and psychological changes take place. It's an involuntary response that increases our heart rate, breathing, blood pressure and metabolism. The increased blood to your muscles prepares you to fight or escape.

It is part of our evolution that people with the best flight or fight reactions are more likely to live long enough to have children and so continue the human race.

The reaction we experience can help us cope when dealing with situations such coming under attack from another person or some other kind of predator but in the modern world, it's not that helpful to react to every uncomfortable, awkward or threatening situation by getting into a fight or escaping.

Fighting with your neighbour after they've asked you to turn the sound down or to stop Rover from leaving little presents on their lawn etc is not likely to lead to a harmonious relationship. In some circumstances, the flight or fight response kicks in when it is not needed and physical symptoms will appear. Our hearts will pound, our breathing will increase rapidly, our muscles will become tense and our mouth will dry up. This will probably be accompanied by headaches.

In addition, our thought processes will become stressed and our minds will race. A stream of unhelpful thoughts along the lines of "I'm going to fail", "I can't cope", "I'll make a fool of myself" or "Everyone can see me blush" will kick in. This will result in our feelings becoming confused, panicky and frightened.

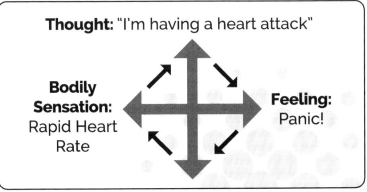

Thought: "I'm having a heart attack"

Bodily Sensation: Rapid Heart Rate

Feeling: Panic!

All this will probably bring about a change in our behaviour. We may run away to avoid the situation, or we may become aggressive. We might end up self-medicating using drink or drugs to soothe our minds.

These factors all inter-relate and in some circumstances, they can develop into a vicious circle which prolongs the stress and makes it worse.

In the example mentioned the person notices their heart rate has increased. This results in them thinking "I'm having a heart attack". The result is they panic and increase their breathing which causes the heart rate to rise even more. This convinces them that they are having a heart attack. This panic state of mind causes them to pay a lot of attention to every physical change and reaction to the point that even a small change seems significant. Around it goes in a vicious circle.

This pattern of response can develop into a panic attack resulting in the individual hyperventilating. The panic sets in resulting in the person thinking they are on the verge of death.

Hyperventilation

When we hyperventilate (breath too quickly) we end up with too much oxygen and not enough carbon dioxide in our blood which contributes to the range of physical feelings we have. One way of dealing with hyperventilation is to breathe into your hands and then inhale and exhale. This sorts out the imbalance of carbon dioxide and oxygen in the blood, and so slows down the hyperventilation.

There are many symptoms of stress and anxiety in addition to those mentioned earlier, including:

• Poor concentration.
• Fear of negative things happing to those you love.
• Feeling over-anxious and upset before doing something.
• Stopping doing things that you have done before.
• Feeling fearful of things, but can't pin down the reason.
• Feeling on edge.
• Disturbed sleep.
• Believing your friends don't like you.
• A fear of death.
• Feeling anxious about tomorrow, next week, your future.
• An inability to relax.
• Erratic thought patterns.
• The idea of being sociable creates fear.

What Makes You Stressed?

Reading those last few pages may remind you of different occasions where you've found yourself in distress or feeling anxious. Take a look at the worksheet on page 67 and fill in your

What makes you stressed?

What situations make you feel stressed?	
How do you deal with the stressful situations you encounter?	
Which of the techniques in this book do you think will help you deal with stress?	
How might the techniques listed in the book make you feel better?	
Do you use any exercises to lower your levels of stress? If so, which ones?	

"When I came out of the abusive relationship, I slept for most of the first two weeks, I was violently sick, had huge migraines and couldn't eat much. I lost three stone in three months, I was exhausted, stressed and felt alone.

I realised that the abuse I'd endured for several years was responsible for my behaviour, my anxiety, my depression, my lack of sleep and the nightmares I still endured. Learning about how the adrenalin in our bodies responds to intense situations such as violence or other forms of abuse worried me. I grew concerned about how much stress my body had been put under.

Towards the end of the abusive relationship, I felt I had become emotionless and almost robotic as I had learned to shut down.

I remember when I was in that relationship I went to see a consultant about some headaches I had been having and they thought it was linked to a health condition. I left the appointment having been informed I was suffering the headaches because I was hyperventilating due to my breathing too fast. Looking back, I can see that it was my body's way of coping with anxiety and fear. My body had taken over the response without me even knowing about it."

JG

own answers. Are they similar to the situations and responses mentioned earlier? What do you do to relieve the stress?

Regaining Control Through Relaxation

Relaxation, like many things that are worthwhile, is an art requiring plenty of practice. Learning to relax has huge benefits for your physical and mental health. The power of relaxing your body at will is one of the best ways of gaining control of your mind. Whilst resting, you will find tension will drop from the mind and in its place will come improved confidence, calmness, courage and greater strength.

A tense body accompanies a tense mind. A body completely

relaxed helps the mind to relax. There may have been a time when relaxation was spontaneous but for most people these days it must be re-learned.

The object of these exercises is to make relaxation a habit that replaces the tension habit. Breathing should be quiet and easy at all times. In learning relaxation, there is a tendency to allow the breathing to become too shallow and the circulation of the blood too slow. Graduated deep breathing exercises will free tension. It has a calming and steadying effect on the nervous system.

The importance of learning to relax cannot be overstressed, for fatigue and sometimes even pain will follow if muscle tension persists. Muscular tension is not limited to the body. Nerves carrying messages from the brain to the muscles and back will not relax if there is no peace of mind because the muscles are rioting.

It is useful to learn not to over contract your muscles in the activities of daily living as this builds up a pattern of tension. You'll need to think frequently, at odd moments during the day, what tension habits are you indulging in.

Relaxation can be practised sitting in a chair or lying down. It is preferable to have your eyes shut whilst doing these exercises. Of course, if that is too difficult, feel free to keep them open. Take care of any pre-existing physical conditions that make some of the exercises difficult and do not try anything that will cause you pain or distress.

Relaxation Of Arms

Settle back as comfortably as you can. Let yourself relax to the best of your ability (pause). Now, as you relax like that, clench your right fist, just clench your fist tighter and tighter and study the tension as you do so. Keep it clenched and feel the tension in your right fist, hand, forearm (pause) and now relax.

Let the fingers of your right hand become loose and observe the contrast in your feelings (pause). Now, let yourself go and try to become more relaxed all over. Once more, clench your right fist really tight, hold it and notice the tension again. Now let go, relax, straighten your fingers out and notice the difference once more (pause).

Now repeat with the left fist. Clench your left fist. Clench your left fist while the rest of your body relaxes: clench that fist tighter and feel the tension. Relax and feel the difference. Continue relaxing like that for a while.

Clench both fists tighter and tighter. Now with both fists tense, forearms tense, study the sensation (pause) and relax. Straighten out your fingers and feel that relaxation. Continue relaxing your hands and forearms more and more (pause). Now bend your elbows, tense them harder and harder and study the tension feelings. All right, straighten out your arms, let them relax and feel that difference again. Let the relaxation develop. Once more tense your upper arm, hold the tension and observe it. Straighten the arms and relax. Relax to the best of your ability. Each time pay close attention to your feelings when you tense up and when you relax.

Next, straighten your arms, straighten them so that you feel the most tension in the muscles along the back of your arms, stretch your arms and feel that tension (pause) and now relax.

Get your arms back into a comfortable position. Let the relaxation proceed on its own. The arms should feel comfortably heavy as you allow them to relax. Straighten your arms once more so that you feel the tension in the triceps muscles, straighten them. Feel that tension and relax.

Now let's concentrate on pure relaxation in the arms without any tension. Get your arms comfortable and let them relax further and further. Continue relaxing your arms even further. Even when your arms seem fully relaxed try to go that extra bit further, try to achieve deeper and deeper levels of relaxation.

The Facial Area, Your Neck, Shoulders And Upper Back

Let all your muscles go loose and heavy. Just settle back quietly and comfortably. Wrinkle up your forehead now, wrinkle it tighter, and now stop wrinkling your forehead, relax and smooth it out. Try to picture the entire forehead and scalp becoming smoother as the relaxation increase.

Now frown and crease your brows and study the tension. Let go of the tension again. Smooth out the forehead once more. OK, close your eyes tighter and tighter. Can you feel the tension?

Relax your eyes. Keep your eyes closed, gently, comfortably and notice the relaxation. Now clench your jaws, bite your teeth together, study the tension throughout your jaws. Hold that for a second, now relax your jaws.

Let your lips part slightly, appreciate the relaxation. Press your tongue hard against the roof of your mouth. Look for the tension. All right, let your tongue return to a comfortable and relaxed position. Next purse your lips, press your lips together tighter and tighter (pause) and relax the lips. Note the contrast between the tension and relaxation. Feel the relaxation all over your face, all over your forehead and scalp, eyes, jaws, lips, tongue and throat. The relaxation progresses further and further.

Onwards to your neck muscles. Press your head back as far as it will go against the chair or floor and feel the tension in the neck; roll it to the right and feel the tension shift, now roll it to the left. Straighten your head and bring it forward, press your chin against your chest. Let your head return to a comfortable position and study the relaxation.

Let the relaxation develop, shrug your shoulders, right up. Hold the tension, drop your shoulders and feel the relaxation. Neck and shoulders relaxed, shrug your shoulders again and move them around. Roll your shoulders up and forward and back. Drop your shoulders again and relax. Let that relaxation spread deep into the shoulders, right into your back muscles; relax your neck and throat and your jaws and other facial areas as the pure relaxation takes over, then grows deeper and deeper.

Chest, Stomach And Lower Back

Relax your entire body to the best of your ability. Feel that comfortable heaviness that accompanies relaxation. Breathe easily and freely in and out. Notice how the relaxation increases as you exhale. Breathe in and hold your breath. Study the tension. Now exhale, let the walls of your chest grow loose and push the air out automatically. Continue relaxing and breathe freely and gently. Feel the relaxation and enjoy it.

With the rest of your body as relaxed as possible fill your lungs again, breathe in deeply and hold it again. That's fine, breath out and appreciate the relief; just breathe normally. Continue relaxing your chest and let the relaxation spread to your back, shoulders, neck and arms. Merely let go and enjoy the relaxation.

Now let's pay attention to your stomach area. Tighten your stomach muscles by breathing out, make them hard. Notice the tension and then relax. Let the muscles loosen and notice the contrast.

Once more press and tighten your stomach muscles. Hold the tension and study it and then relax. Notice the general wellbeing that comes with relaxing your stomach. Now draw your stomach in, pull the muscles right in and feel the tension this way. Then relax again. Let your stomach out.

Continue breathing normally and easily and feel the gentle massaging motion all over your chest and stomach. Now, pull your stomach in again and hold the tension. Push out and tense in that position, hold the tension. Once more pull in and feel the tension, then relax your stomach fully.

Let the tension dissolve as the relaxation grows deeper. Each time you breathe out, take note of the rhythmic relation both in your lungs and in your stomach. Notice how your chest and your stomach relax more and more. Try to let go of all contractions anywhere in your body.

Direct your attention to your lower back. Arch up your back, make your lower back quite hollow and feel the tension along your spine. Now settle down comfortably again relaxing the lower back. Just arch your back up and feel the tension as you do so. Try to keep the rest of your body as relaxed as possible. Relax your lower back, relax your upper back, spread the relaxation to your stomach, chest, shoulders, arms and facial area, feel those parts relaxing more and more.

The Hips, Thighs And Calves Followed By Complete Body Relaxation Exercise

Let go of all tensions and relax pause for a second then flex your buttocks and thighs. Flex your thighs by pressing down your heels as hard as you can. Relax and note the difference. Straighten your knees and flex your thigh muscles again. Hold the tension. Relax your hips and thighs. Allow the relaxation to proceed on its own (pause). Press your feet and toes downwards away from your face so that your calf muscles become tense. Study that tension (pause). Now relax your feet and your calves (pause). This time

74

bend your feet towards your face so that you feel the tension along your shins. Bring your toes right up, relax again (pause) keep relaxing for a while.

Relax your feet, ankles, calves and shins, knees, thighs, buttocks and hips. Feel the heaviness of your lower body as you relax still further. Now spread the relaxation to your stomach, waist and lower back. Let go more and more. Feel that relaxation all over. Let it proceed to your upper back, chest and shoulders and arms and right to the tips of your fingers.

Keep relaxing more and more deeply. Make sure that no tension has crept into your throat, relax your neck and your jaws and all your facial muscles. Keep relaxing your whole body. In a state of perfect relaxation, you should feel unwilling to move a single muscle in your body. Think about the effort that would be required to raise your right arm. As you think about raising your right arm see if you can notice any tensions that might have crept into your shoulder and your arm. Now you decide not to lift the arm but to continue relaxing. Observe the relief and disappearance of the tension.

You should now become conscious of your limbs going to sleep, a reluctance to move because it seems harder to do so. You should be aware of automatic breathing which is the ONLY movement of the body.

Now you can become twice as relaxed as you are by taking in a deep breath and slowly exhaling. With your eyes closed so that you become less aware of objects and movement around you, thus preventing any surface tensions from developing, breathe in deeply and feel yourself becoming heavier. Take in a long, deep breath and let it out very slowly. Feel how heavy and relaxed you have become.

Relax And Take A Break

You should try to drop all troubled thoughts and think only of pleasant things. Can you recall some happy memories, the sound of the sea or picnics by the river? Perhaps walking through a field or valley on a summer's day.

Think only of pleasant sounds, the humming of bees, the songs of birds, soft music and dancing. Think of calm moonlit nights, the lapping of waves and the peace and stillness all around. Now just lie quietly for a few minutes.

Only when you feel you are rested should you bring your muscles into action. Stretching as before but this time think of your muscles as being strong and powerful. That yawn as you breathe out should be one of satisfaction. Turn onto your side and stretch your arm. Now roll over onto your hands and knees and get up slowly.

Exercise - The 7/11 Breathing Technique

All forms of mental distress involve high emotional arousal states such as anger, anxiety or depression. Breathing exercises are one of the ways of relaxing the body and mind, which will enable the states of anger, anxiety and depression to lessen.

One simple breathing technique that is perfect for restoring a sense of control through reconnecting us with our rational brain, whilst lowering blood pressure is the 7/11 breathing technique.[3]

Inhale to a count of seven and exhale to a count eleven.

This method will have an immediate beneficial effect on both your physical and psychological wellbeing. Exhaling the carbon dioxide stimulates the parasympathetic nervous system which is responsible for calming you down.

When relaxed you can't be anxious because you cannot experience two contradictory states simultaneously.

This week try and practice a breathing/relaxation technique and record in your thought diary how it goes.

"Taking some time to do the relaxation exercises made me realise the benefits I could have if I used them when I am feeling overwhelmed. For me, it is about giving myself permission to take control of any stressful situation I find myself in."

JG

Thought Diary

Date	Situation	Emotions	Automatic Thought	Challenges?
		What were you feeling?	The first thought you had?	Is there a challenge to the thought?

WEEK FIVE
Our Children

How did the relaxation practice go? Did you try the 7/11 breathing? You'll probably found that the 7/11 breath technique is a lot simpler to do than it sounded. The benefits of oxygenating your brain through exercise cannot be stressed too often. If only we had learned about breathing exercise when we were children. If it feels unnatural just keep practising. The benefits will be enormous and we recommend you try and build some regular relaxation into your week.

The Affects on Children and Parenting Skills

This is potentially a difficult chapter to read because I am asking you to consider the impact that living in an abusive relationship has had on any children you may have. If you don't have children this chapter is still useful to read because it explores the effects that living in an abusive relationship has on others. However, if as a parent you have had your child removed permanently or a child has died, you may wish to skip this chapter altogether.

As a parent, you may have done all you could to hide what was happening from your children. You may have thought they were upstairs and asleep in bed or at the grandparents or out of the house when any shouting or violence was taking place. I'm afraid that all the evidence gathered from speaking to children tells us that they always know what is going on. It is a myth that children who don't see the direct abuse are not traumatised by it.

Learning that a child is aware of abusive behaviour can be quite painful and hard for the abused parent to take on board. I must stress at this point that what I am saying doesn't mean you didn't try your best to protect them. It's really important that you remember that the person responsible for the impact on any children is that of the abusive partner.

Impact On Children

Children can suffer from abuse, whether they are being directly targeted by the abuser or not. The abuse can take many forms including those listed below:

Intimidation

An abusive parent can create fear in the child through actions, gestures and violence towards them or the other non-abusive parent. For a child witnessing cruelty to a household pet, a parent or another sibling, the negative effects can be overwhelming.

Enforced Isolation

A child or young adult can suffer from becoming isolated. For example, if the abusive parent stops the child's friends or family members from visiting or vice versa. The abuser may have reduced the amount of time the child could spend with the non-abusive parent.

Emotional Abuse

Children can suffer as a result of emotional abuse such as name-calling, shaming, or using the child against the other parent. In this scenario, the abusive parent may persuade the child to tell them about what the other parent is up to when the abuser is not around.

Economic Abuse

Using bribes, withholding pocket money, using a child as a bargaining chip, spending family funds and withholding basic needs for a comfortable life.

Threats

The threat of physical harm, abandonment or confinement to the child or their non-abusive parent or sibling will cause the child emotional and physical stress.

Belittling

Punishing the child by ignoring the child's wishes or needs, interrupting the child when they are speaking and treating the child as a servant will also do untold damage to the child.

Misusing Authority

Threatening to embarrass or punish using institutions such as the courts, the police and school. Using the threat of punishment by God, another relative or a person in authority.

Other areas of abuse include: committing incest, sexual touching including kissing, twisting arms, pushing, pinching, kicking, hitting, sexualising a child's behaviour.

Moving Forward – A Healthier Approach To Children

Children should experience love and care from a parent and the best ways of expressing this are through improving and growing trust and respect between the parent and child.

As a parent, you must respect their feelings and believe they are telling the truth. It is also essential to give them as much independence as possible within safe limits. Children have the right to their own feelings, needs, wants, who they make friends with and to take part in whatever (safe) activities they may decide to enjoy.

A non-abusive parent will provide their child with clothing, housing and food. They'll also teach their child all the things they need to feel secure as they grow such as personal hygiene and what makes a healthy diet. It's also important for healthy parenting to take the time to be part of the child's life outside the home by attending events, supporting them in sport's days and other school activities.

Ensuring that the child is aware that they are safe and that they can express themselves will bring about positive results in your child's development. As a parent, you need to show that you are someone who is dependable. You will probably show a great deal of affection for your child, continue this by being attentive and affectionate when something goes wrong for them.

Always be consistent when laying down rules for your child; this consistency will teach them to recognise healthy boundaries.

Most children will know when you are suffering, this includes if you are suffering from ill-health. This can add to their sense of insecurity. It is much easier for the child to feel secure if they know that their parent is looking after themselves.

Exercise

This week I want you to think about one of the issues mentioned in this chapter that affects your relationship with your child/ children. If you don't have children, you can think about what it was like for you as a child.

Did any of the issues mentioned in these pages affect you? Try to explore what options you have to address these issues. Keep them simple. There is usually a simple solution to any problems you encounter.

They may not have seemed that simple when you were in your former relationship but seem relatively easy, now that the relationship has ended. It's also a good idea not to overload yourself with too many changes all at once. We have included a checklist of things, that you could do with your child /children, which can help strengthen your relationship with them.

It's important to spend small amounts of quality time with your child. Of course, parenting is not an exact science, and there's no such thing as the perfect parent. Don't forget to record what you can in your *Thought Diary*.

I have also included a list of positive things to do with your children, which are all suggestions to help them develop their own resilience as well.

Thought Diary

Date	Situation	Emotions	Automatic Thought	Challenges?
		What were you feeling?	The first thought you had?	Is there a challenge to the thought?

Children's Activities

Can you...?	How did it go?
Tell your child you love them?	
Spend time with your child doing what they want?	
Sit with them and let them talk to you - ask them how they are feeling?	
Give them clear boundaries without shouting at them e.g. sitting in one place while having their tea?	
Allow them to be cross with you if you are wrong?	
Help them with self-directed work without either doing it for them or getting cross if they can't do it?	
Tell them when they have done something good?	
Play games they want to play?	
Cook meals for them and engage them in cooking with you?	
Praise them for being them?	

Checklist of activities to enhance relationships with children

What were your thoughts?

"I nearly didn't do this part of the programme because I felt overwhelmed with the shame and guilt. I'm their mother and I felt I should have protected them. I now recognise that I tried to do this in my own way.

My children were two and four years old at the time and I thought they were so young that the abuse I endured wouldn't have made a difference to them. How wrong I was.

Recognising that the abuse had not only affected me but had also affected my children gave me a large lump in my throat. I remember learning about how abuse to an adult can harm any child and affect their development.

I had worked hard to keep the abuse away from them but I couldn't avoid acknowledging the negative effect being in that relationship had on them. It became apparent that they not only witnessed the abuse I had endured but they had and were going through the abuse as well, they were victims too.

There were patterns of behaviour I had adopted to defend myself from abuse, that I continued to follow after I had left the abusive relationship. Things that may seem small, but still lingered like a bad habit.

For example, when my children asked me for anything I would say 'let's check with daddy first'. Eventually, they didn't ask me if they could do an activity or go somewhere they would say 'can we ask daddy if we can…'.

At the time my son was almost mute and now I can see that the pair of them were too well behaved for children of their age. I should have seen that it wasn't the normal pattern of behaviour for children."

JG

WEEK SIX
Self-Care

Welcome to Week Six. Have you written about the issues covered last week in your *Thought Diary*? And, if you have children of your own did you manage to spend small amounts of quality time with them? Of course, it's hard to get quality time with children especially if it's not what they feel they need. At times all children can be focussed on everything else but their own parent(s).

Self, Not Selfish.

So here we are looking at self-esteem again. It's such an important subject and deserves a lot of attention. This week we'll revisit some of what we've talked about in previous weeks and add some more information about our core beliefs and self-esteem.

Remember what we've already discussed? You've learned that the inner, often hidden and unconscious beliefs you have about yourself will affect your self-esteem and self-worth. These beliefs are known as your core beliefs.

We need to understand the effect these core beliefs have on our self-esteem and self-worth. Keep in mind that, put simply, our positive core beliefs result in positive self-esteem and negative core beliefs result in low self-esteem.

For example, if you say or think something along the lines of "I am no good", it will result in your not valuing yourself. This perceived lack of value will result in your not challenging any abuse you suffer and at worst you will believe that you are getting what you deserve.

At this point, your self-esteem will be shrinking and you'll be triggering your Negative Automatic Thoughts (NATs). These

NATs can cancel out any positive thoughts you may have had or any positive statements that someone else has said about you. Think about how, when someone pays you a compliment, you brush it away. Your response is set to automatic.

Examples Of Negative Automatic Thoughts

A friend says: "Your hair looks nice".
Your response: "Oh I washed it this morning but it needs a cut" That's an unconscious Negative Automatic Thought suggesting something like "it's a mess because I'm a mess?"

Your mother says: "You look great in the jacket you're wearing" **Your response:** "It's just a cheap old thing I've had for years". That's an unconscious Negative Automatic Thought suggesting something like "it has no real value, and therefore I have little value".

Another friend says: "You did really well in that quiz" **Your response is:** "I'm not as good as so and so" That's another unconscious Negative Automatic Thought, but this time it's suggesting "I'm not as intelligent as so and so?".

Ridicule By An Abuser

An abuser will often ridicule and challenge the abused partner's core beliefs. Unfortunately, because it is often the case that abused victim is isolated and because of this there is no opportunity for the abused person to check out their beliefs with the help of friends or relatives, it becomes impossible to differentiate between the core beliefs of the abuser and the person they abuse.

Challenging The Negatives

Look at your *Thought Diary* and try and identify ways that can help you identify the Negative Automatic Thoughts that affect you. Of course, mulling things over and over in your head, especially Negative Automatic Thoughts, can add to your anxiety. With that in mind, I am going to tell you how you can take positive steps so you're not just sitting and reflecting on these thoughts in your own home.

One of the things that I want you to do this week is to try and become aware of occasions when someone says something positive or nice to you and you dismiss it! You can think of the examples listed previously. Then I want you to record it in your Thought Diary and consider what the underlying thinking is that is triggered by a negative core belief.

Part of what I am asking you to do is to become more 'present' in your interactions with others. I am not, as that may sound, suggesting that you usually only interact with others on a superficial level. Most of us have several levels of interaction, from the intimate to the superficial.

For instance, when we say "Good Morning!" to a shop assistant or passersby, it is usually only on a superficial level compared with how we interact with partners and family members. That superficial level is perfectly ok and should be seen as an appropriate level of interaction, especially when we consider all the interactions we may have with all kinds of people throughout the day.

However, what I am suggesting here is that because of the abuse you have experienced, there has been a change in your core beliefs. Your negative 'internal dialogue' triggered by NATs, may mean that even trivial interactions with others can be painful.

I'll give you a fictional example: Yesterday I visited a local shop where I vaguely know the person on the checkout. I smiled at them when it was my turn to be served and as usual, we exchanged a few pleasantries. When I visited the same shop today, that person hardly spoke or acknowledged my presence. My NAT response was to leave the shop wondering what I might have done wrong.

Is this feeling, that it was somehow my fault that they acted like that, something you recognize for yourself?

The feeling I was experiencing is my inner dialogue reinforcing a negative perspective. What I am going to encourage you to do is replace your inner negative dialogue with a positive one.

Dialogues Within – Negative And Positive Inner Chats

We all have an inner dialogue chatting away throughout the day. Perhaps it feels like it is silent, especially if we are relaxed and paying attention to something else other than ourselves. But in reality, it is ongoing.

The dialogue can be negative, for example, "I am stupid" or positive "I'm clever". It is often slightly more sophisticated and we also try to qualify what is said, even when we are expressing positive thoughts. This latter part may well be our NATs attempting to underplay a positive achievement or positive statement. It could be our NATs attempting to add some sort of rider i.e. "I am willing to work hard to overcome the abuse", whereas thinking "I have worked hard to overcome the abuse" which is more positive.

Affirmations

What's an affirmation? An affirmation is a short statement that once learned and repeated over a period of time helps us reprogram the mind. They are proven methods of self-improvement that are especially useful when dealing with negative thought patterns. The word itself comes from the Latin *affirmare*, which means to strengthen. Affirmations will help change the inner dialogue from negative to positive.

The successful use of self-affirmation as a tool to help with healing has led to scientific researchers investigating if changes can be seen in the brain when individuals use positive self-affirmation techniques. According to research studies using Magnetic Resonance Imaging (MRI) machines have provided evidence that suggests that there is an increase in some neural pathways when an individual practices self-affirmation techniques.

"The pre-frontal cortex-involved in positive valuation and self-relate information processing, becomes more active when we consider our personal values". This means that the more an individual practices a series of affirmations the more likely it is that the individual will believe what is being said and the more likely it is that they will change the way they think about themselves. The researchers results suggest that those who use these self-affirmation techniques are more likely to view information as "more self-relevant and valuable". [1]

Here are a few simple affirmations:
• I am learning how I want to be treated.
• I have learned a lot about myself.
• I like myself and I deserve to be well treated.
• Today, I am brimming with energy.

90

"At first, affirmations were difficult but once I got going they flowed out of my hand and onto paper. Below are some of my original affirmations:

I have a supportive partner and two beautiful children who are the key to why I can carry on.

I am starting a new job and this will help us financially and me personally.

I have a new life growing and it will bring us joy, some closure and remembering in a more positive way.

You may be able to see I struggled with these at first. The affirmations were more about others in my life and what I am working towards. I noticed this upon reflection and recognised that I struggled to be positive about myself.

Again with this work in progress, and my recognising that this is a result of my low self-esteem, I knew that I needed to work on positive self-talk.

After a couple of years my affirmations changed:

I can choose which path I take.

I am free to express myself in whatever way that is and I will be comfortable in my own skin.

I believe in my skills and abilities.

I'm getting stronger every day.

I have the power to change my story.

As can be seen, there's a clear difference between the two different times. I believe these will continue to improve as my life continues. Positive self-talk has helped with dealing with my Negative Automatic Thoughts. It's important for me to recognise that it was the whole 'me' that I have needed to work on."

JG

- Happiness is a choice, I base my happiness on my own accomplishments.
- Today, I am leaving my old habits behind and creating new ones.
- My fears are fading away.
- I am putting the past behind me.
- I am concentrating on the future.
- I know and trust myself.
- The more I like myself the more others like me.
- I accept myself, I respect myself, I respect others.

Exercise

Think up four different affirmations, write them in the boxes on the exercise sheet and practise them three times this week. If you need inspiration take a look at Jennifer's list or the sample suggestions mentioned earlier in the chapter. It is also a good idea to do them in front of a mirror. Write about how you get on in your *Thought Diary*.

What's an affirmation?

An affirmation is a statement that something you already do or plan to do is positive
For example:
"I have broken away from the abuse I have lived with and I am now moving forward in my life"
"There is nothing to fear. I have a lovely safe home"

Think of at least four affirmations of your own and write them below

1

2

3

4

Thought Diary

Date	Situation	Emotions	Automatic Thought	Challenges?
		What were you feeling?	The first thought you had?	Is there a challenge to the thought?

WEEK SEVEN
A New Assertive You!

How was last week's exercise? Don't tell me, you felt a little silly talking to yourself in front of a mirror. No surprises there as I think we all do at first. When people start practising their affirmations in front of the mirror they often say how silly they feel and how difficult it is to do. Don't worry if you feel silly, it's just part of being human and will still bring you benefits when it comes to affirming. Were you aware of not dismissing a compliment if you received one? It's hard not to and it takes a fair amount of practice just to say 'Thank you'.

Expressing Emotions

Remember I suggested that those who are still in abusive relationships should avoid using this book. I'll explain. Within an abusive relationship you, and/or any children, may have adopted passive behaviour in order to appear as non-confrontational as possible.

It is important to stress that if you were still living in an abusive relationship any attempts to be assertive in your behaviour, as outlined in these pages, may have produced dangerous results for you. Hence the warnings.

Learning to be assertive may be difficult at first. You may be tempted to look back and wish that you had behaved differently in the abusive relationship. Don't wish that you'd been more assertive whilst in your abusive relationship. Being assertive at the time would not have changed much and you would only have put yourself at greater risk.

However, now that you are no longer in the abusive relationship, I want to ask if you ever find yourself in situations where you want to say something, but don't, in order to avoid having a row or confrontation of some kind? Perhaps the opposite response is true, you get so angry about something that you have a violent outburst and regret it afterwards? These are examples of when and where proper assertive communication would have helped. I will reinforce that being assertive with your partner would not have stopped the abuse. Remember being either assertive or aggressive with your abusing partner wouldn't have stopped the abuse, in fact, it would have likely increased your risk.

It is really important that you recognise that you behaved in the particular way you did whilst in the abusive relationship in order to keep yourself and any children safe. Learning how to be assertive or any other new skill is only possible because you are now safe.

Being assertive while in an abusive relationship is potentially very dangerous. Even if your ex-partner never physically assaulted you, it is quite likely that you were aware that to challenge them would have escalated their need to control. This need could have easily led to a physical assault.

Why Is Assertiveness Useful?

A lack of assertiveness in our lives can affect our relationships and our quality of life as we are unable to communicate effectively and so end up not getting what we want, need or deserve. Unfortunately, family life, career prospects and stress levels can all be affected by a lack of assertiveness.

Luckily, if you carefully examine how you communicate with others, there are a number of ways in which you can begin to assert yourself, helping to improve your quality of life.

So what do we mean by assertiveness?

The Cambridge English Dictionary[1] describes the word assertiveness as "the quality of being confident and not frightened to say what you want or believe". Another definition describes being assertive as "the flexible pursuit of having our preferences met, our opinions voiced, our emotions and beliefs honestly communicated in an appropriate way at the relevant time".[2]

In order to be truly assertive, you need to see yourself as having worth and a right to enjoy your life without unwarranted hindrance. Also, you will value others equally, reciprocating their right to an opinion and to enjoy themselves.

This view enables you to engage respectfully with other people, whilst also respecting your own needs. Being assertive will help protect you from being hurt or used. Many people find it difficult to communicate honestly, directly and openly with other people all the time. But it is possible most of the time and certainly, it exists in any healthy relationship.

Assertiveness Involves The Following:

- Being clear about what you feel, what you need and how it can be achieved.
- The ability to communicate calmly without attacking another person.
- Saying 'yes' when you want to, and saying 'no' when you mean 'no' (rather than agreeing to do something just to please someone else).
- Deciding on and sticking to clear boundaries – being happy to defend your position even if it provokes differences.
- Being confident about handling conflict when it occurs.
- Understanding how to negotiate if two or more people want different outcomes.
- Being able to talk openly about yourself and being able to listen to others.
- Having confident, open body language.
- Being able to give and receive positive and negative feedback
- Having a positive, optimistic outlook.
- Not always getting what you want.

Compare being assertive to the two other ways of relating to others - passive behaviour or being aggressive.

Passive Behaviour

This kind of behaviour typically involves:
- Being overly 'nice'.
- Being submissive.
- Being afraid of conflict and social rejection.
- Keeping opinions and feelings to yourself.
- Wanting to win others 'approval'.
- Feeling frustrated and angry inside.
- Feeling not understood.

- Being unable to express own needs.
- Never getting your own way.

It is easy to see how in an abusive relationship this type of behaviour is necessary. But you can also see how this type of behaviour means bottling up your feelings and emotions. Earlier in the book, I explained how living in an abusive relationship can result in depression, anxiety and the use of substances to get you through the day because of bottled up emotions.

Remember, in an abusive relationship adopting a passive mode is usually a risk management strategy used to protect yourself and any children. You probably had to give in or remain silent. Continually having to be passive and deny how you really feel will have been a huge contributor to the emotional distress you endured.

Aggressive Behaviour

Alternatively, you might have developed aggressive behaviour as a response to the abuse you received. This kind of behaviour typically involves:
- Bullying
- Intimidation
- Being manipulative
- A lack of empathy or caring about other people's opinions, feelings or desires
- A desire to dominate others, and using threats and/or verbal and physical displays of power to achieve this.
- Always getting your own way

Assertive Not Aggressive

One of the myths about assertive behaviour is that it involves being aggressive. This isn't true. Assertiveness involves clear, calm thinking and respectful negotiation within any space where each person is entitled to their opinion. Aggression can result from bottling up feelings which eventually explode, leaving no room for healthy communication.

Sometimes, when coming out of an abusive relationship, you can find yourself see-sawing between aggressive and passive behaviour. This can be a reaction to finding yourself in a situation

98

where you no longer have to bottle up your feelings and emotions but, after months or perhaps years of having to deny your own feelings, emotions and needs, they can all come spilling out in a bit of an explosion.

This may be the same for any children you have. While this recognisable pattern is understandable, taking out your justifiable anger on others, who are more than likely innocent parties, is not acceptable behaviour. Whereas, taking the time to learn to be properly assertive is much more likely to get your needs met.

Assertive Not Selfish

While some people think that being assertive is about being selfish in some way, it is in fact, the opposite. Assertiveness is about acknowledging all opinions as important. An assertive attitude states "I matter and you do too". Learning how to express yourself assertively can seem daunting at first. Thankfully, there are many things you can do to learn to become more assertive.

Body Language

Thinking about body language is essential when it comes to learning to become more assertive. It's useful to express yourself using open, non-threatening body language. How you are seen by others will influence how they respond to you.

If you adopt a stance that includes clenching your fists, legs apart and an unflinching glare, then those you are dealing with will themselves feel threatened, fearful and or aggressive. If your stance is very passive, with your shoulders hunched and no eye contact, then this too might be seen in a negative light. An assertive person will usually stand in a relaxed upright manner, looking calm with some eye contact.

Exercise

You can do this in front of a mirror or if you have a friend that would be able to help you, you can try this exercise with them.

The idea is to try out the different types of posture and body language as you imagine being aggressive, passive and assertive. Think of the signs of passive and aggressive behaviour we mentioned earlier.

See what it feels like to change from being in a passive or aggressive stance to using more assertive body language. You can record your observations in your *Thought Diary* so that when you look back in the weeks ahead you can see any changes in your thinking when you do adopt these changes.

You'll notice that just standing in a confident, calm way can feel empowering. If you are practising with a friend ask them to tell you what they observe about the changes in your posture and how it makes them feel as well. Jot their observations down in your *Thought Diary*.

Communication

Another aspect of being assertive is the way in which we communicate. Clear communication is important, this is where we show the following:

• Knowledge – you can understand and summarise a situation.
• Feelings – you can explain your feelings about a particular situation.
• Needs – you can explain clearly what you want or need, giving your reasons and you can articulate any benefits to the other party.

Early on, as you practice being assertive, you'll see from this list that you may need to prepare for new situations. So, before you go into a situation where you will need to be assertive, think about the following points:

• Be honest with yourself, especially about your own feelings.
• Keep calm and stick to the point.
• Be clear, specific and stick to the point.
• If you meet objections, keep repeating your message whilst also listening to other points of view. Try to offer alternative solutions if you can.
• Don't forget to ask if you are unsure about something.
• If the other person tries to ignore what you have said, then, without being confrontational and repeat what you have said.
• Use non-threatening body language.
• Always respect the rights and point of view of all those involved in the conversation.

"Whilst in the abusive relationship I had let my abusive ex-husband walk all over me. Unfortunately, this pattern didn't stop with him. It felt as if people could see I couldn't say no to anything and as a result, I would agree to do anything in order to go along with the flow.

At the time I didn't want to upset anyone. Rarely did I tell anyone if they had hurt my feelings as I was always worried to do so would lead to conflict.

Looking back at my behaviour it seemed that I was very passive and I longed to be assertive. I struggled with standing up for my desires, values and opinions. I had a lack of confidence. I wondered if I was going to be able to grow more confident and recognise I had value.

Saying no is one of my biggest challenges, but having the list of assertive skills in front of me helps me to focus.

I remember when I first said 'no' a few weeks after this part of the programme. I celebrated, for once I didn't feel bad at all. In fact, saying 'no' empowered me.

I recognised that making these changes wasn't going to be easy but my Bill of Rights and affirmations underlined that fact that I was worth it and that I needed to continue to give it a go.

I find it most difficult to be assertive with my family members. I still feel that I don't want to upset and let them down in some way.

I had been worried that practising assertiveness was going to use up more energy, leaving me exhausted, and I was worried as to whether or not I was going to make it through the coming week.

But I also wanted to see if I possessed the power to actually use all this new knowledge to action what I was learning. It's easy to read and utilise it... but implementing it can feel completely different."

JG

- When planning what you'd like to achieve by being assertive you may need to write down what you want.

Exercise

For this week's exercise, I want you to think of a situation where you want to be assertive. You will need to practice. At the end of the chapter, there is a list of suggested areas you could try plus a checklist to fill in.

This is potentially a big change and it means that to be assertive you need to be able to do the following:
- Accept your rights.
- Say how you feel.
- Decide what is appropriate and fair.
- Express your views.
- Ask for what you want.
- Accept responsibility.
- Negotiate and compromise, where appropriate.
- Say NO.
- Give compliments.
- Give constructive criticism.
- Handle criticism.
- Tackle put-downs.
- Do things you enjoy.

Of course, don't expect to do all the things listed from the word go. Indeed, there are always times when being assertive is hard. It also true that at times part of being assertive is having the confidence to be able to decide not to be assertive.

What Do You Want To Change?

At Home

The relationships with the people you live with, the jobs and the roles of those living in the home.

At Work

The relationships with your boss and your workmates. The way you deal with authority figures, customers, service users, strangers etc.

Your Friends And Family

How do you get on with parents, siblings, good friends and acquaintances?

Social And Community Events

How do you get on at or in groups, meetings, parties, pubs, restaurants, outings and holidays?

Draw up a list of areas in your life you want to change for the better using assertiveness. You can list four or five things that are fairly easy to do. For example, to say 'no' after being offered overtime or asked to do babysitting. To be more affectionate with family members.

Fill in the worksheet on the following page to find out about your patterns of behaviour.

Identifying behaviour

In the boxes below write down some of your own patterns of behaviour

Identify and give a couple of examples of social situations where you feel uncomfortable	
Give an example of behaviour which you think would be seen as inappropriate in a social situation	
Give an example to show what you have learned from this book that could help you change your attitudes/feelings and actions/ behaviour to participate effectively in social situations	

Thought Diary

Date	Situation	Emotions	Automatic Thought	Challenges?
		What were you feeling?	The first thought you had?	Is there a challenge to the thought?

WEEK EIGHT
Being Angry

Your abuser did not have difficulty expressing their anger.
What they did was deliberate. They used aggression and
violence to control you so they could have power over you.
They did not have a problem with anger management. This is
important to remember as we look at anger as an emotion.

Welcome to Week Eight. How did the exercise go? Did you explore being assertive? It will boost your confidence and grow a more assertive you if you do practice. Like with any form of learning, the more you practice the more you will benefit. Did you encounter any problems?

Perhaps the negative words of your abusive former partner keep coming to haunt you. Is the voice of your former abuser still preventing you from moving forward? If so, don't worry too much, the more you practice, the more assertive you will become and the more that voice will fade.

This week we're going to continue looking at assertiveness, in addition to exploring how best to deal with anger.

Angry With Others?

If you've lived in an abusive relationship you have every right to feel angry toward your abuser for the way you were treated. You may also feel anger towards those you turned to for support whilst you were in the abusive relationship. Perhaps, for whatever reason, they didn't give you the help you felt you needed.

These people might be family members or friends, they might be the agencies who you thought would be able to help; the police, social services and others, who didn't seem to understand what was going on or appear to listen to what you needed. It is worth noting that anger is often a secondary emotion and the primary or underlying emotion behind it, is actually something else such as fear or frustration.

Angry With Yourself?

However, while feeling angry is understandable, without the right knowledge to help you deal with your anger, there is a risk that you will have turned the anger towards yourself.

While you were in the abusive relationship you may have swallowed your anger for the sake of some peace. You will have developed mechanisms for hiding your anger as a way of keeping yourself and any children safe. This response, while understandable given the circumstances, will have meant your denying your anger.

You may have used this coping strategy so that your partner could not use it as an excuse to be abusive towards you or any children. This could mean that you adopted unhelpful coping strategies such as self-harm, depression and misuse of substances, to feel normal.

Alternatively, you could have found yourself turning your anger towards others such as your relatives and outside agencies. Unfortunately, in doing so, you may have alienated yourself from the very support that may have been there to help.

Expressing Anger Safely

While all the responses mentioned can be understood and your right to feel angry is undeniable, expressing it in a way that is safe and will not harm anyone, including yourself, will be one of the most valuable assets in your recovery.

Everyone feels angry sometimes, yes even those people you know who appear to be calm under all circumstances, feel anger. Anger is a normal human response to feeling threatened or frustrated, and because it is normal, it would be surprising that you do not feel angry when you think about your abused past or certain aspects of it.

However, if that anger is not well managed, it can become a problem, threatening your new relationships with any children, friends, family or colleagues. Anger left unchallenged can potentially affect every aspect of your life.

To manage your anger, you need to learn how to express those
108

feelings in as healthy a way as possible. In doing this you will see that anger becomes a helpful, controlled reaction to everyday frustrations.

What Is An Anger Problem?

Anger is an emotional state that varies in intensity, ranging from mild irritation to violent rage. Like other emotions, it is accompanied by chemical and physical changes in the body, including increased adrenaline levels and an increased heartbeat. Is it a useful emotion? The answer is yes, possibly more so when we need to run away from danger. This understandable response to danger is known as 'flight or fight'.

The increase in levels of adrenaline and focus can help us escape, but for day to day use it is also useful. Some people are able to express their anger in a controlled and constructive way, whilst others lash out in an aggressive, uncontrolled manner, either immediately or after their feelings about something have built up over a period of time. They "explode".

This explosive pattern of anger management can lead to violent or bullying behaviour which endangers other people and property. As mentioned earlier, anger can also lead to self-harm.

If you feel that your anger is out of control or you are having difficulties appropriately expressing the anger you feel about your past, you will benefit from addressing how you handle your angry feelings.

As I have explained above, you have every right to feel angry about what you underwent as a result of the behaviour of your intimate abuser.

Your intimate abuser did not have difficulties expressing their anger. What they did was deliberate. They used aggression and violence to control you so they could have power over you. They did not have a problem with anger management.

On the other hand, you, as the target of their anger and abuse, will not have been able to express yourself in a healthy constructive manner because of their abusive control over you.

Strategies

Thankfully, there are a number of healthy strategies for dealing with anger. I say thankfully because we all need to deal with angry feelings and find ways to express them which are not harmful to ourselves or others.

Sometimes it can help to think about how it feels in your body as you start to feel angry; Where do you feel it? How do you visualise it? What does it feel like? Once you have recognised this – next time it happens you can put one of the strategies in place before the anger spills out in a way that is harmful to you or others. There are many techniques to try, find one that works for you.

So, if you feel anger rising within yourself, don't let it build up until you are on the verge of rage. Take a slow deep breath and allow you heart rate to decrease. This will have the effect of reducing the flight or fight response. Now, close your eyes (if appropriate) and repeat the word 'relax' as you breathe in and out.

Giving yourself time to think is essential. You may be starting to feel angry because of something someone has said or done. Instead of responding immediately it may be necessary to pause, give yourself time to reflect on the situation. It may be as simple as taking a breath or if need be removing yourself from the situation that is upsetting you.

Talking things through with a friend or colleague will probably help calm your anger. Try and think logically about the cause of your anger. Think about how the situation that has made you angry may be related to your former abusive relationship. Has it reminded you of something that used to happen when you were being abused? Remember, at the time, you were being controlled and manipulated by your abuser. You didn't have the options or choices you have now.

Consider if there is a misunderstanding and if you are really angry about this current situation or something else such as your past experiences.

Learn How To Express Yourself Calmly

As a result of being humiliated, belittled etc over a long period of time, you may find yourself over-sensitised to potential criticism and may overreact or respond to things that you wouldn't have before or read things into what people to say to you based on your previous experiences.

Try to express your feelings in an assertive manner, using

calm, logical words. If you are having or expect to have a heated discussion, it is best to be prepared to keep the following in mind:
• Slow down – think carefully about what you want to say
• Try to think what it is that is underlying the anger you are feeling
• Be clear about what you are asking for and how it can be achieved. Try using phrases like 'I feel angry with you because…'
• Listen carefully to the other person and remember that everyone is entitled to their opinion
• Keep your cool in the face of your own and the other person's anger
• You may feel offended if you are being criticized. Try not to be put off by this and keep listening
• Be patient and ask questions to get to the heart of the problem
• Try to be carefully assertive rather than sarcastic or aggressive

Grounding

Grounding is a particular type of coping strategy that is designed to immediately connect individuals to the present moment. Grounding is often used as a way of coping with flashbacks or dissociation. Because of its focus on being present in the moment, grounding can be considered a variant of mindfulness.

It can also be a method of distraction to help individuals cope with upsetting thoughts, memories, or feelings. Grounding techniques often use the five senses; sound, touch, smell, taste, and sight. Different techniques work for different people.

Sound

• Turn up the radio or listen to your favourite song.
• Talk out loud about what you see, hear, or what you're thinking or doing.
• Call a loved one.
• Put on some nature sounds such as birds chirping or waves crashing.
• Read out loud.

Touch

• Hold an ice cube and let it melt in your hand.
• Put your hands under running water.
• Take a hot or cool shower.

111

"Anger for me is very difficult because when I was in the abusive relationship I would take it out on myself. I couldn't argue back so I would shut down. This could lead to me responding by self-harming and having a panic attack.

I remember a time when my ex-husband proceeded to wind me up and I completely lost my ability to let what he was saying go over my head. He had worked me into such a state, that I didn't know what was right and wrong or what he actually wanted me to do.

I screamed at him to make some sense. I ended up kicking the side of the bed with the result that he looked at me with utter disgust and told me I was insane.

My frustration with his response led to me banging my head repeatedly on the floor. I had lost control, all my anger came out and I ended up harming myself. This resulted in me having a headache and a lump like a huge egg on my head.

I began to recognise he was playing mind games with me. I didn't know that this pattern of abusive behaviour had a name. My abusive (ex)husband was gaslighting me.

I should have known better because his next move was to continue to use this method of control against me.

In general, I didn't have a problem with anger, but it did anger me when he wound me up and confused me with my reality. My natural response was to shut down or look for a way to escape.

At the time I could contain my anger and frustration for long periods. Unfortunately, after sustained abuse, it would eventually pop. Usually, my anger builds because someone doesn't give me the chance to have a voice and it makes me feel very frustrated. This behaviour, which reminds me of my former abuser, can then trigger an angry response.

I now know that I need to be able to talk about how I feel and that those feelings shouldn't be ignored. I not only want to be listened too, I also want to be understood and for the other person to show empathy, just as I'll try to do for them."

JG

- Rub your hand lightly over the carpet or a piece of furniture, noting the texture.
- Massage your temples.
- If you have a dog or cat, cuddle and pet him or her.
- Drink a hot or cold beverage.

Smell

- Sniff strong peppermint, which also has the benefit of having a soothing effect.
- Light a scented candle or melt scented wax.
- Get some relaxing essential oils and smell one.

Taste

- Bite into a lemon or lime.
- Suck on a mint or chew peppermint gum.
- Take a bite of something spicy or peppery.
- Let a piece of chocolate melt in your mouth, noticing how it tastes and feels as you roll it around with your tongue.

Sight

- Take a mental inventory of everything around you, such as all the colours and patterns you see. Saying them out loud is helpful too.
- Put on your favourite movie or TV show.
- Play a distracting game on your tablet, computer, or smartphone.
- Complete a crossword puzzle, sudoku, word search, or other puzzles.
- Read a book or magazine.

Other Suggestions To Cope With Anger

- Regular exercise can help to prevent the accumulation of tension and can also give you regular time away from everyday stresses.
- Relaxation exercises such as yoga and meditation will also help you to release any tension in a controlled and healthy way. You can find out more from your GP, local library or health centre.
- Try to keep your alcohol intake within the daily recommended intake (2-3 units for women and 3-4 units for men). Alcohol lowers your inhibitions, which in turn can trigger angry behaviour.

- Change your environment. It's great to find alternatives for those situations which add stress to your life, and it's important to schedule in time to relax and unwind. It doesn't take a long time, but if you timetable in regular times to relax, you'll find everyday stressful situations, become less of a burden.
- Learn to express yourself, either by chatting to friends or learning to express your feelings in another way. Perhaps you may enjoy expressing how you feel in a creative manner through art or writing.

Hopefully, you can see that managing your anger healthily and productively also involves using those assertiveness skills we explored earlier in this book. I do think you have a justified reason for being angry, but discharging that anger constructively and responsibly will enable you to move forward in your life and not be held back from making new relationships with friends, partners and others because they won't be put off by your anger.

Exercise

Over the next few days think about some of the ways you can lessen everyday stress. Take a look at the suggestions mentioned in this chapter. Which of those appeal to you? Think of some of your own.

It's a well-known fact that undertaking exercise, even a short ten minute walk, can reduce stress in everyone's life. Is there a yoga class, swimming club or some other form of exercise that's available in your area that you could sign up to do? Try and reduce the amount of alcohol you drink as excess alcohol is not the solution to stress. Take any opportunity you can to chat with other people.

You don't have to entertain them or prove how amazing you are. A simple hello to an elderly person in the street can be enough to give you a mood boost. But, don't worry if they don't respond. It's not any fault of yours and it doesn't mean they don't like you (they don't know you anyway).

Use your *Thought Diary* to take note of how you feel when you get back from doing some exercise, or trying a new grounding technique.

Thought Diary

Date	Situation	Emotions	Automatic Thought	Challenges?
		What were you feeling?	The first thought you had?	Is there a challenge to the thought?

WEEK NINE
Boundaries

D id you manage to do last week's exercise? Perhaps you went on a quick walk or tried a yoga class? If not, don't worry. Exercise can seem like a daunting prospect if you've not been doing it on a regular basis. But once started it is something to treasure. It gives you a mood boost and often helps with perspective.

If you kept your thought diary after the activity did you notice any negative thoughts stopping your activity ? Maybe something your abuser might have said? Are you still keeping a daily record of your mood ?

Creating Boundaries – Keeping Yourself Safe

This week we're going to be looking at what we need to do to keep ourselves safe and protect those we love. How do we do this? In general, we keep ourselves safe and make positive life choices by being aware of our boundaries and expectations.

Our boundaries set the limits for acceptable behaviour in the people around us. The quality of these relationships depends on the strength of our boundaries. Think about the following questions:

1. How do people close to you treat you?

2. Do they take advantage of your good nature?

3. Do they leave you feeling guilty?

If you answered 'yes' to any or all of those questions, there may be a need to reset your boundaries. Your boundaries are a measure of self-respect and it's vital to set them at a level that feels comfortable to you.

Our boundaries develop as we grow and as young children, we learn them from our parents, school teachers and others as we start to interact with the world we inhabit. Firstly at home itself, then through our interactions with the world outside the family home, such as school, clubs and playgroups.

We learn about appropriate behaviour such as personal space, non-intimate and intimate touching, the use of appropriate language and behaviours in different settings as we develop. We also grow to understand how to treat and respect others and they, in turn, learn how to respect us.

Personal boundaries both protect us and attract others. Weaker boundaries can leave us more vulnerable, taken for granted, abused or damaged by others. A healthy self-respect that says 'I deserve better than this' protects us from exploitative relationships and from the pitfalls of loving those that may not have our best interest at heart.

Also, having clear personal boundaries helps protect us from people who waste our time, who take without giving, who tell us their problems and never listen to ours, who put us down, remind us of our failures, lay guilt trips on us, blame us for their failings and who dump their anger on us, be they friends, partners, parents, siblings or colleagues.

Remember, having vague boundaries will attract people who may want to use you. Whilst, clear boundaries will attract people who are more likely to respect you and care about you.

It is likely that as a result of your time in the abusive relationship, your boundaries will have changed and been undoubtedly compromised. Now that you are free of that abusive intimate partner you have the opportunity to re-establish and remodel your boundaries to meet your current needs.

Out With The Old

As you have now left your abusive partner your boundaries may need updating to reflect who you are now. You will find the process of reaffirming or resetting your boundaries empowering. If you were once willing to spend chunks of your working day helping out colleagues, but now can't find the time, you can replace the boundary that says 'I want to please' with one that says 'I value myself and expect others to do so as well'. Boundaries are not only useful in our personal lives but also in our professional lives as the example below demonstrates:

118

Lisa is a self-employed fitness instructor, who set up new boundaries for her clients. She identified the people who regularly changed appointments at short notice. She explained to them that losing the appointment at short notice meant she was losing money and this was threatening her livelihood.

As a result of setting clear boundaries, of the clients she identified, 50% subsequently honoured their appointments, 25% agreed to pay cancellation fees and the remainder made no further appointments. Thanks to her setting a clear set of boundaries Lisa was earning the same money as previously and had more free time.

Of course, whilst setting boundaries we must be sure they are not too strong otherwise they can prevent good things from entering our lives.

For example: David said his goal was to find a better-paid job before he could marry his partner. Though it was obvious he enjoyed being a graphic designer and could live comfortably on his salary, he feared that he was not able to give enough support to his partner Claire, and because of this fear he was afraid she would leave him.

David's response came from the fact he had been hurt in a previous relationship and as a result, he put up barriers to protect himself from the pain of another rejection. Thanks to counselling David learned to accept that love doesn't come with a guarantee. He also learned to relax his boundaries and he and Claire have now been married for two years. David still works, doing the job he enjoys.

The Price Of Moving On

Keep in mind, some of those close to you may have a vested interest in you staying just the way you are. They may find it convenient to have someone on call for tea and sympathy all day. Perhaps they need someone who is fatter, thinner, poorer or more stressed than they are for them to feel better about themselves. Remember that every life change has a price tag attached.

When you establish new boundaries, you may lose people you thought of as close to you along the way. Be assured that every relationship worth having will survive you resetting your boundaries.

Emotional Boundaries

A successful and healthy emotional relationship between two individuals, whether intimate or not, will exist if each has a clearly defined sense of their own identities. Without our understanding of who we are and what makes us unique, it will be difficult to engage in the process of an ongoing fully functioning relationship.

Though living in a functioning relationship is not always smooth, all healthy relationships have their ups and downs, the relationship itself is a safe environment that generally enriches each of the partners. We need a clear sense of self in order to clearly and unambiguously communicate our needs and desires to our family, friends or partner.

A healthy sense of self is based on how you work with and understand your own emotional boundaries. These boundaries allow you to protect yourself from manipulation. This will also make it possible for you to separate your own thoughts and feelings from those of others and to take responsibility for what you think, feel and do.

When you have a greater understanding of yourself it is more likely that you will feel safe in an intimate relationship. You will not feel threatened by the intimacy of the relationship. You'll also grow to love, appreciate and respect your family, friends and partners as individuals.

Although it is true that similarities often bring two people together it is also true that within a healthy adult relationship, respect for differences is as important as it encourages the growth of each partner.

Childhood Boundaries

Unhealthy boundaries can result from being raised in a family where the need to develop personal space and individuality were not properly understood. If as a child you were not nurtured in a way that enabled you to develop a healthy ego and a healthy sense of who you are, then it can be much harder for you as an adult to understand the need for boundaries but also how to apply them.

You may have unconsciously and incorrectly learned that boundaries don't matter, that you as an individual human being, don't matter except where you are useful for the emotional needs of others.

120

This may have happened because you lacked the support you needed from your parents to help you form a healthy sense of your own identity. This lack of sense of self will also have been learned or reinforced whilst living in an abusive relationship.

The abuser may have commented and/or criticised everything about you. This would have meant you had to develop behaviours in order to seek the approval and praise of the abuser. Adopting this approach would have helped you to feel safe from either emotional or physical abuse.

Boundaries Set By Your Abuser

Many individuals who have left abusive relationships will carry with them boundaries that were adapted or changed in order to survive the abuse they experienced, effectively continuing to carry the abuse despite their having left the abusive relationship.

If we are not careful this restricted pattern will continue into any future relationships such as those with new partners, friends and even those relationships we have with family members. In effect, you will continue to try to please others while denying your own needs.

As with surviving an abusive relationship, carrying all this with us means we can end up compromising our boundaries and we end up doing anything it takes to make the relationship work. This just repeats the negative and restrictive patterns left over from the abusive relationship.

Setting Your Own

The best and most rational answer to all this is to find out who you are and what makes you unique. You don't need to be in a close intimate relationship to benefit from finding out.

You may think things are good enough as they are or you may irrationally believe that you don't deserve any better. Perhaps you feel that your life is meant to be like this; full of sacrifice and putting everyone else's needs first. You may be giving up not only your life dreams but your sense of worth to maintain your safety and to remove your fear and anxiety of being abused again.

You need to be aware that a healthy relationship is one in which boundaries are not only strong but flexible enough to allow you and the other person to flourish with your uniqueness. A sense of respect on the part of both individuals should allow each to be equal, have respect, share different opinions and have no need to impose or use emotional or other pressures to bend the will of the other person.

Healthy boundaries allow trust and security to develop in a relationship because they offer an honest and reliable framework by which we can get to know each other. If we don't know where our self ends and the other begins it is going to prove to be impossible.

A Feeling Of Responsibility And Guilt

One of the characteristics of being in an abusive relationship is the feeling of guilt that you may have adopted. This feeling, whilst not correct, is understandable especially if your abuser made you feel responsible for their failure or unhappiness.

The abuser will have intended you to feel guilty resulting in your lowering your boundaries to be available to them at all times. As a result of being made to feel guilty for your abuser's mistakes, you may have tried to help them by rescuing them from the consequences of their actions. You may have done this to prevent their anger at failure being directed at you or any children.

No Rescues

The healthiest way to deal with this with a new non-abusive partner is to show them respect whilst letting them succeed or fail on their terms. Support them by all means but don't rescue them. If someone does ask for help, take a pause and ask yourself a couple of questions before you answer them.

Firstly, is the help needed something they can do themselves and secondly, do I resent giving my time, money or resources to help?

Within your abusive relationship, it is quite likely that you were conditioned to rescue others and this will also have been a way for you to stay safe. Of course, in a healthy relationship, you'll want to comfort or encourage your partner when times become difficult and you will want to rejoice with them when they are successful.

When you have developed healthy boundaries you'll be able to say "I trust and respect you to make your own life choices. As my

122

equal partner, I will not try to control you nor take away your life choices."

A Genuine Love

Compassion is a worthy quality, but alongside sympathy, it can be confused with love especially where boundaries have been eroded. Enjoying healthy boundaries will lead to respect for the other individual and equality in the relationship. These are healthy features of mature love. When one partner is in control there is no room for the give and take of a healthy relationship.

A Fantasy

Many abused individuals often fantasise that things will get better someday. They may even believe that the reason for the abuse is down to bad luck and that someday in the future they and their abusive partner will resolve any issues and all will be well.

Of course, there are good days, where there is little abuse, and that can lull the abused into a false sense that things will improve for the better. These feelings are often encouraged by the abuser saying that 'it won't happen again', 'it's because of stress', 'it's because of alcohol' and so on; all excuses for the abusive behaviour.

It's possible that you portrayed to others the myth that you were in a perfect relationship and you may have believed it yourself. Denying and minimising the reality of an abusive relationship are common ways for individuals to cope with the horror of what is happening.

You may have ignored the abuse, manipulation, imbalance and control in the relationship and by doing so you were unable to confront them because of fear, threats, intimidation etc. Of course, the fantasy of a happier future rarely, if ever, comes to pass.

Whilst in the abusive relationship it may be the case that believing in the 'fantasy' could have kept you safe or alive and was simply another way of coping with the horror of your situation. When problems are present in a relationship, good boundaries will allow you to define the problems and to communicate with your partner in finding solutions. They also encourage and promote a healthy self-image and trust.

Exercise

Think about how the different people in your life treat you and how you treat them. How do people close to you treat you? Do any of them take advantage of your good nature? Do they use humour to put you down? Do they leave you feeling guilty if you aren't able or just don't feel able to volunteer to do the thing they ask?

Think about your own desires. Do you ask anything of other people? Remember, it's ok to ask and it is ok to be asked. It is also ok to say no or for someone else to say no to you. This is part of respecting our own and other's boundaries. Record your reflections in your *Thought Diary*.

"When I started this session on boundaries I thought it was going to be about restrictions. All the boundaries that I had known were there to describe things I could and couldn't do. Also, my ex-partner didn't respect any of my boundaries. He didn't respect things I did or didn't like. If I asked him to stop doing something that for me was upsetting, he would ignore my request.

There were times I found it difficult to explore the things that had happened to me in my abusive relationship. I continued to suffer from the abuse because I still had to deal with my abusive ex-husband.

Speaking to my new partner, family members, school officials, domestic abuse support workers, my solicitor, the family court and the Children and Family Advisory and Support Service, about him and his abuse meant his influence was inescapable. I needed time to think about other things.

Following a chat with my new partner about this programme, and in particular the need for boundaries, we decided to use what we call 'the banana method'. If I was tired or didn't want to talk about a particular thing, I would say 'I don't want a banana split, thank you'. This meant that it was then my responsibility to come back to him to continue the conversation. This method helped me to engage with someone I needed to build trust with. It was the start of my journey to learn that I can put boundaries in place and be in control. In turn, my partner could also use it with me. Understandably, my partner didn't want to talk about it all the time either.

A few months later I decided I needed to create my own boundaries or methods to deal with people I didn't want to enter a major conversation with. These would usually be people that upset me and were bad for my emotional state. In the past, I would have been polite and entered into a conversation, but now I didn't want to put myself through it anymore.

I have several reasons I use to control a conversation, from 'I am in a rush to get to a meeting' to not answering my phone. It may seem rude but I am protecting myself and it also makes me feel that I am in control. It was a boundary and response I adopted to protect my mental health.

I now see the boundaries I set as something positive, that can help me. They have become a healthy part of my life."

JG

Thought Diary

Date	Situation	Emotions	Automatic Thought	Challenges?
		What were you feeling?	The first thought you had?	Is there a challenge to the thought?

WEEK TEN
Grief and Loss

You've now arrived at Week Ten...Fantastic! Have you noticed any changes? Following last week's exercise did you notice how you interacted with other people? Did anyone ask you to do them a favour and did you turn them down? If so, how did you feel?

You will have found that those that respect you will have taken your answer in a positive manner and gone elsewhere to find help. And this will not have had any kind of negative effect on your relationship with those people. Those that did not respect your boundaries and choices will have found it hard to deal with you saying "no", and they may have been cross or difficult with you for not doing what they wanted. As hard as it might be you may be better off without these people in your life until they can respect the new you with healthy boundaries.

This week we'll explore the possible losses that someone who has endured intimate partner abuse may have experienced following the ending of the relationship. These kinds of losses can be both practical and psychological. Although to some these losses may not appear as understandable as those experienced following the death of someone close to you, the feelings of loss experienced following the end of an abusive relationship often mimic the same stages of grief like that experienced by a bereaved person.

We are going to look at the impact such grief can have on an individual after they have ended an abusive relationship. As you will know all relationships start in love and some of the psychological losses, will still cause upset and distress. It is not that unusual for an individual to have loving memories of their abusive partner.

Multiple Losses

It is also true that you may have lost more than just a partner. As with bereavement, it may be the case that there are other losses connected with your former abusive partner's family through broken relationships or destroyed bonds. Make a list of all the things you may have lost when the relationship ended.

Perhaps you may be experiencing grief having lost shared friendships, contact with children, neighbours etc. If you have had to leave the family home and neighbourhood in order to protect yourself, all those small, less intimate relationships you may have built with people who worked and lived in that area may have become strained or even ended.

You may also be mourning the loss of your self-respect, sexuality and self-identity. All the losses mentioned here all add up and are important to you as an individual.

While recovery can mean that many of these losses can be reclaimed it may still be important for you to allow yourself to grieve appropriately. It is also useful to be able to acknowledge that some of these relationships were necessary whilst you were in the abusive relationship for your protection and that of any children.

During an abusive relationship, you will have made choices about your lifestyle and relationships based on fear and intimidation. With hindsight, it is not uncommon to look back and think that you may have made mistakes. Making judgements in error and poor choices when it comes to dealing with families, relationships, money, jobs, friends etc is something we all do throughout our lives.

For most of us, the effect of those choices is not catastrophic. But, being in an abusive relationship forces us to make decisions that have an impact on those around us. Once out of this relationship, it is possible for you to repair any damage done by the decisions that were made while living under duress.

Psychologists dealing with those experiencing loss and grief, such as that encountered following bereavement or those who have left an abusive partner, recognise that there are five stages of grief. I have listed these stages with brief descriptions many of which you will probably recognise. [1]

128

The Five Stages Of Grief

Denial

This is the first of the five stages of grief. Denial is the conscious or unconscious refusal to face facts, absorb information or deal with reality, relating to the situation concerned. It's a perfectly natural defence mechanism. It may appear easier at times for you to look back at the abusive relationship you have left and deny the reality of what took place. This is perfectly understandable as that may well have been how you coped with the situation you found yourself in at the time.

Anger

The anger you feel can take many forms and you may be angry with yourself or others. It is not unusual for those who have been through what you have experienced to be angry with others, especially those close to them. As we have already said feeling angry is perfectly normal, it's where you direct it that is important.

Bargaining

Individuals facing serious trauma can try to bargain or negotiate a compromise. For example, many people will ask their ex-partner, "Can we still be friends?" when facing a break-up. Bargaining in this manner rarely provides a sustainable outcome, especially when dealing with an abusive partner where it may also be dangerous.

Of course, it should always be remembered it is not possible to bargain or deal with an abusive person in this way as they will always want to be in a position of power.

Depression

It's natural to feel sadness, and regret, fear and uncertainty, etc when leaving an intimate partner, even one who is abusive. Depression can set in as a form of preparatory grieving, much like that felt by someone facing the loss of a loved one with a terminal illness. It's the dress rehearsal or the practice run for the 'aftermath' of separation.

This stage will mean different things to different people depending on who it involves. It's a sort of acceptance with emotional attachment.

These feelings are an indication that you are accepting the reality of the situation you find yourself in. However, this form of depression is different from clinical depression, which is the type of depression needing medical or supervised psychological help. Of course, this kind of depression can also appear after many years in an abusive relationship.

Being depressed in the manner described here is about being sad. Although you may feel elated that you are free of the abuse, you may be surprised to feel sad about it too. This is simply your response to a feeling of loss about what might have been.

Acceptance

Although broadly speaking acceptance is an indication that there is some emotional detachment and objectivity about what has happened or is happening to you. This is your opportunity to see the abusive relationship for what it truly was, which in turn will result in your no longer feeling any emotional attachment to your abusive ex-partner.

Sadness about the loss of love, the loss of dreams, the loss of times that were good, the loss of your partner is normal. However, it does not mean you have made the wrong choice.

Exercise

Think about what you've had to give up now the abusive relationship has ended, look at the list you made earlier. Now make a list of all the things you have gained since the relationship ended. What did you gain? Often the losses are material (home/status/car) and the gains are more emotional (piece of mind, security, friendships). What, if anything, do you miss? Make a note of your thoughts in your diary, and as usual, try and spot if they are NATS and if they are representing the voice of your abuser.

Thought Diary

Date	Situation	Emotions	Automatic Thought	Challenges?
		What were you feeling?	The first thought you had?	Is there a challenge to the thought?

"One of the reasons I felt I couldn't leave my abusive partner was because of the possessions I would probably have had to leave behind if I decided to leave, especially those that had sentimental value.

Week Ten of the programme reminded me that I had already lost friendships and family as a result of the relationship with my abuser. I hadn't been to my home town in more than two years and all my relationships had either become strained or were lost.

After leaving him I lived in fear and so I got rid of our mutual connections on social media, even if they were friendships I had formed to begin with. We also had a dog called Molly and sadly I had to leave her behind.

To this day I don't know what happened to her. There are times I miss her because during the time I lived with my abuser walking the dog had given me a good reason to get out of the house.

I also had a finance deal on an expensive furniture suite and I'd known there were several months of outstanding payments that needed to be met. What hurts is the loss of those possessions, especially those that had been given by someone like my late aunt.

At first glance, it may seem that I have lost more as a result of leaving the abusive relationship, certainly less than I have gained. This is not the case as I have regained my freedom, my ability to make choices, the chance to repair strained relationships and a great deal of control over my life.

It's difficult to talk about all this because it feels like I am spending energy on thinking about what's been lost than what's been gained. I've spent a massive amount of energy focusing on trying to rebuild my life. I now know that the expensive suite I left behind doesn't matter. In hindsight, I wouldn't have wanted the memories attached to it anyway."

JG

WEEK ELEVEN
Healthy Relationships

ollowing last week's chapter did you think about what you'd lost when your relationship with your abuser ended? Comparing what was lost with the freedom you've gained will show you that you've done the right thing. Most material possessions you've lost can be replaced.

Sadly, some sentimental possessions may have been lost forever, but as you'll probably agree, your abuser controlled the amount of time you had to enjoy them. You've reclaimed your time as your own, now you can enjoy new experiences and posses items that are truly you own.

Creating Healthy Relationships

The penultimate week focuses on how to recognise the warning signs within any future relationship. It is a disturbing and unsettling fact that once an individual has experienced one abusive relationship they are thought to be vulnerable to another.

This week we discuss the common characteristics of abusive individuals and encourage you to identify your most vulnerable areas and to look at how you might mitigate against them in the future.

Experiencing an abusive and/or violent relationship does not mean that you shouldn't have the expectation (or the right) to form new healthy adult relationships. However, the experience of abuse may have left you vulnerable to those who seek to control their partners. This is due to the possibility that your experiences of abuse may have affected your understanding of what constitutes an unhealthy/healthy relationship.

WARNING SIGNS!
What Makes An Unhealthy Relationship?

Forming and maintaining adult relationships based on mutual trust, love and respect is not as easy as you may think. You may find that because of what you have been through it is difficult to define exactly what a healthy relationship is.

To help with this we'll first take a look at what an unhealthy relationship is and how to spot it.

1. Individuals who are possessive and/or over-controlling about how and where their partners spends their time.

2. In the early stages of a relationship, this can appear as flattering, but if they start to call or text you in an obsessive manner it can soon become an unhealthy form of possessiveness.

3. Jealous partners tend to be possessive and controlling. They appear to dislike your friends and family, finding fault with them and in some circumstances, they may try to stop you from seeing them.

4. Abusive individuals typically try to sweep partners and potential partners off their feet. They may try to rush partners into sexual relationships, perhaps pressuring their partners to move in with them and/or to get married.

5. Another problem with abusive individuals is that they may lie. It's a real risk as these predatory individuals are often pathological liars and may even lie when there is no reason to do so.

6. They can also be quite secretive even with those they are supposedly having an intimate relationship with. There may be gaps in time when they are unaccounted for or phone calls where they won't say who they are talking to.

7. Abusive individuals are usually opinionated, with male abusers it often concerns traditional (read antiquated) male/female roles in the home along with other beliefs supporting the dominance and authority of men in relationships with women.

8. The abuser may put their partner down in subtle ways, perhaps belittling their opinions or beliefs. A bad temper often goes hand in hand with this form of abuse.

9. Many abusive individuals are explosive and are triggered

easily. Warning signs are when there are stories about individuals being aggressive with someone else? Or they are seen acting that way? Or, they are seen acting that way. Have you seen or heard them being verbally abusive to someone else? Restaurant staff/cab drivers? This kind of behaviour can be a major cause for concern.

10. Abusive and overly aggressive people tend to blame others for the mistakes they make and this includes those who are abusive within an intimate relationship. They find it almost impossible to take responsibility for their own mistakes.

11. Some abusers get unduly rough during sex in the name of 'fun'. Intimate moments will only take place on their terms. Often they will make partners feel uncomfortable about their own needs. It has little to do with shared intimacy and more to do with abusive control.

12. What about drug or alcohol use? While 80% of heavy drinkers do not abuse their partners, there is a definite link between alcohol or drug misuse and domestic abuse. Alcohol does not cause the violence but disinhibits the already abusive individual. Violence, while the perpetrator is under the influence of drugs or alcohol, is generally of a more severe nature.

13. Abusive individuals may have a reputation. Perhaps they've cheated on a partner in the past, perhaps they've got a reputation for being unreliable. It may be the case that their relationship with a former partner is unhealthy or they are unable to show any form of empathy with a former partner. These can all be signs of an unhealthy individual who may be abusive.

14. An abusive partner will often act differently in company. This difference can manifest in them being distant or dismissive. Of course, it can also be the other way round, at home they may be distant but when in company they can appear appreciative and affectionate towards you.

15. Abusers often ignore privacy. They may open email and mail. They check phone messages. They can be invading privacy by checking social media profiles or telephone messages. They may monitor friends and how individuals communicate feelings to others.

Remember these are predatory individuals who can be extremely charming, witty and fun to be with. One of the reasons many abusive individuals are capable of being so charming is that they may have no trouble giving others compliments that are exaggerations or lies.

This overt flattering and attentive behaviour sometimes referred to as 'love bombing' also serves as a 'grooming' process to reel us in. We feel incredibly lucky to have met this person and may remain in the relationship long after it becomes abusive in an attempt to recreate these first few weeks. With this in mind, it is probably sensible to be wary if they are extremely complimentary before they know you.

Risk Areas

Look at the list of warning signs and have a think about where you might be vulnerable if you start a new relationship. If you have been on your own for a while the excitement of meeting someone new and falling in love is intoxicating. However, think about the warning signs. If you know that you have got involved very quickly in the past think about going a bit slower - don't introduce the new person to your children for say three months.

A non-abusive person will not find this difficult, in fact, they will respect the way you are protecting your children. A potentially abusive person will try and get you to shift your boundaries to suit them - remember the last chapter!

The Positive Signs To Look Out For
In A Healthy Relationship?

When one considers the points made in the previous paragraphs, spotting good signs may sound difficult. Of course, even healthy relationships can indeed suffer from some of the points raised earlier. A good definition of a healthy relationship is one based on equality, has balance and benefits both partners.

Partners in healthy relationships will come to understand that support is there in times of need. A healthy relationship is built on trust, it is not rushed, and is open and honest. You will know that the relationship feels equal and that both partners show each other respect even when they disagree about something. In those

136

circumstances, they either find common ground or let the issue go. Communication and intimacy are very important in a healthy relationship.

Intimacy

Intimacy in a new relationship can be a daunting prospect, especially after having left an abusive relationship where you were made to feel vulnerable and it was used against you by your abuser.

In a truly intimate, trusting, loving relationship, you may reveal yourself or show the real you, making yourself vulnerable without it being used against you. A healthy relationship means you can share secrets and private thoughts.

A relationship of this kind will give you a sense that you have a special, unique and distinct bond between you and your partner. You'll feel a real tenderness towards your partner and they will feel the same towards you. The pair of you will also show each other mutual respect, recognition and approval of each other's need to be a sexual being.

What Can Stop Intimacy?

Those who have left an abusive relationship will know that they bring with them many of the patterns of behaviour they adopted to survive their abuse. These behaviours and responses can understandably lead to blockages when it comes to intimacy with someone new. Unfortunately, these behaviours will probably have resulted in certain beliefs that now make intimacy difficult. Firstly, remember these beliefs may well have been instilled in your thoughts by your abuser.

Below is a list of the possible negative thoughts your abuser might of instilled in you, suggested by James J Messina.[1]

- If I open myself up to another individual, I am bound to get hurt or be exploited.
- People with whom I have been involved in the past have abused, neglected and mistreated me. How can I expect it to be different in the future?
- People have said to me 'I love you' and 'I hate you' in the same

breath. I get so confused. How can I ever believe anyone?
- If you open yourself up to trust someone, they will always take advantage of you.
- I am a worthless, useless, piece of junk. How could anyone ever care about me?
- I am a slut or whore if I enjoy sex.
- A women's role is to be subservient to men in all respects.
- Intimacy means sexuality and sexuality always means sexual intercourse.
- I can take care of myself just fine. I don't need anyone else to clutter up my life.

Do you believe any of these? If so, put them in your *Thought Diary* and working through the questions listed here, see if these were, in fact, thoughts planted in your head by your abuser.

Recognising Intimacy
The statements that follow are recognitions of intimacy:
1. Continuous, honest communication and contact with one another exists even if the contact is not in person but is by letter, phone, e-mail or some other form.
2. A mutual task to carry out at home, school or at work is willingly shared, discussed and enjoyed together.
3. An affinity or attraction to one another exists to the exclusion of others.
4. The company of one another is sought even when you both have a wide selection of other individuals from which to choose.
5. A sense of humour, sense of play and casualness develops in which you enjoy 'give and take' and are relaxed in each other's company.
6. A protective sense of privacy and guardedness about your relationship exists; it is not subjected to public scrutiny, criticism or judgement.
7. The relationship is a productive enterprise resulting in mutual satisfaction, reward and reinforcement for each other.
8. The relationship has a purpose, direction and order to it that is reasonable, realistic and healthy for both of you.

"I was very nervous about this section as I had already entered into a new relationship. I worried that it could be unhealthy for me if I ended up over-analysing things due to my having become very aware of my former partner's abusive behaviour. I was determined not to end up in the same kind of relationship again.

It's easy to identify the differences of an unhealthy/healthy relationship on paper but I wondered if I would spot the warning signs at the start of a relationship? I've learned that these warning signs can be so subtle and hard to spot.

Thanks to this part of the programme I could now see the warning signs that had appeared in the early stages of my former relationship with my abuser. Now, these small glimpses of that early abuse make me wince.

I wrote a huge list of positives describing my new partner including:
- *Honest/Trustworthy*
- *Respectful*
- *Complimentary*
- *Appropriate*
- *Helpful*
- *Financially balanced*
- *Comforting*
- *Challenging- in a positive way*
- *Proud of me/Values me*
- *Protective*
- *Loving*
- *Supportive/Listens*
- *We're both equal*
- *A father to my children*

When I left the man who abused me I didn't know that I would marry again or that I would have another child. I also didn't know that this time it would be a healthy relationship. Because of that former abusive relationship, I didn't think the possibility of a healthy relationship actually existed."

JG

9. A firm commitment, agreement or contract exists with each other to be mutually supportive, understanding and accepting of one another.

Exercise

Firstly, think about your former intimate abuser. When you read the descriptions of the early signs of someone who might be abusive, do you recognise the signs?

Secondly, looking at your current relationships with an intimate partner or a good friend, do any of them show the signs listed? Remember, healthy relationships can have a few of the signs listed so don't worry if your partner suggests having a joint bank account, especially if they are not trying to make you give up your own account or hand over control of your finances.

If you would like a new partner in the future why not write a 'shopping list'. Write down all the attributes you want them to have e.g. good relationship with ex-partners, regular contact with their children, a job, enjoys long walks. Keep the list safe and when you meet someone check out your list. If they don't fit most of them think long and hard about why you might change your mind about what you want.

Thought Diary

Date	Situation	Emotions	Automatic Thought	Challenges?
		What were you feeling?	The first thought you had?	Is there a challenge to the thought?

WEEK TWELVE
The End Of The Journey

D id you think about how your intimate abuser controlled you? With that wonderful thing called hindsight did you manage to recognise the early signs as listed in Week 11? Hopefully, with those relationships you value now you've moved on from your intimate abuser, there are few if any signs. And did you identify your most vulnerable area and how you can get support to manage it in the future?

This final week aims to encourage you to explore what you've been doing using the methods and suggestions contained in this book. Looking back you'll realise you've come along way since you picked it up and started reading.

I suggest that you take a look at what you've written in your *Thought Diary* during that last twelve weeks and if you remembered to keep daily mood scores look to see if they have changed. This is also the ideal time for you to write down how you are feeling now and how true to yourself you feel you are being. You can compare your latest writings with what you wrote about yourself in that first week and over the proceeding weeks.

If you've followed the suggestions I've made in the book and allowed yourself to explore your true feelings and noticed your responses to them, then you will be feeling more in control of your life.

What About The Future?

When you are reviewing your writings and thinking about what has been suggested in the book, it may be that some areas of exploration undertaken in these pages may need revising or you may require additional time. The beauty of this book is that you can easily flip back to the relevant weeks. Re-reading these pages will help reinforce your ability to recognise what happened to you when you were with your abusive partner and the coping strategies you may have adopted to protect yourself in that former unhealthy relationship. New, healthier strategies will have started to become your natural way of dealing with the situations you encounter when communicating and interacting with others.

Of course, it can take time for these new healthier strategies to become your default way of being. As long as your mental and physical health are not deteriorating, then there is no rush.

To help these healthier strategies become embedded I would suggest creating a personal action plan. You can keep it private, just for you. This may mean making decisions to do things differently and for yourself. This is where the assertiveness you worked on in Week Seven comes in use.

Perhaps you want to find work, sort something out for any children you may have, volunteer your time to something you feel strongly about. Maybe you want to study something that you've been interested in for a long time, and it is only now that you have left the abusive relationship that you feel able to explore your own interests. It may be the case that you have dozens of ideas of what you would like to do. Writing them down will help you to focus.

A Personal Action Plan

As I suggested earlier it might be the right time to create your own action plan. This personal action plan can take many forms, from a simple list of desires to a more complicated diary format. I've included a simple form (page 144) that may help you along the way.

Start by thinking about listing what you want to achieve in the short term and then in the medium to long term. Perhaps you want to learn to drive and then buy a car. The short term aim is learning to drive and the long term aim is to buy a car. The possibilities are endless and unique to you.

List the steps you need to achieve this. You can include any organisations you need to approach or individuals you need to talk to about getting help.

Writing all this down will help focus your mind on how you can make these desires take place. For some, you may want to write

144

down how you will know you've achieved what you set out to do. If it is learning to drive, then passing your driving test is an obvious sign that you've achieved what you set out to do.

It is easier to measure success with academic or test orientated plans such as learning a language or learning to drive. Others such as making new friends or meeting potential partners are a little trickier to quantify. But there are signs that you have been successful.

If you go on a course and someone invites you out for a meal, drink, walk etc then that is a sign of their desire to know you better and evidence that you have allowed yourself to become open to new relationships.

Your new strategies, learned with the help of this book, can ensure you avoid the pitfalls everyone faces when doing something new. Remind yourself that usually, the benefits outweigh any pitfalls.

Once you have achieved your goal, take note of how it makes you feel. Reaching one's goals, even the small ones, can help reinforce our feelings of empowerment.

We can learn to trust ourselves and others by following the methods in this book and adopting the healthy strategies contained in its pages. As I suggested earlier, if you are unsure of anything, re-read the specific chapter again.

Use the worksheets contained within the book to add to your learning experience. These worksheets and guides will help reinforce the strategies listed.

Your Action Plan...

	One thing I want to achieve in the next week (short-term goal)	One thing I want to achieve in the next month (long-term goal)
How am I going to achieve this?		
Who will I need to help me?		
How can I make it happen?		
How will I know I have achieved it?		
How does achieving my goal make me feel?		

"Finally, thanks to this programme I can understand what has happened to me and how to work to overcome the negative aspects. I'm starting to feel better about myself and I'm already changing. I'm excited for my future.

During this session, I looked back at the previous weeks. I had come to understand that many people are subjected to the same patterns of behaviour and that no one thinks or knows beforehand that a relationship can be so unhealthy and soul-destroying.

If someone is in a relationship and the behaviour of their partner is abusive they need to understand that the abuse they encounter is not their fault. They also need to understand that their partner's behaviour can't simply be changed by changing themselves.

The programme has completely changed my life and I wouldn't be where I am now, with my positive mindset, health and the awareness I bring.

Completing this programme was a huge achievement for me and I am proud of myself for having done so. At the time I didn't tell the world and I only shared it with those close to me.

If this programme was available to all who had experienced domestic abuse it would free a lot of weight from their shoulders. It would also help prevent others from going into another abusive relationship.

It's not easy being a 'survivor' and no one should underestimate the long term effect. The dictionary definition of the word 'survivor' is a person who copes well with difficulties in their life and this epitomises my belief that however difficult, surviving is worth it on so many levels"

JG

Thought Diary

Date	Situation	Emotions	Automatic Thought	Challenges?
		What were you feeling?	The first thought you had?	Is there a challenge to the thought?

You're Amazing!

Remember what I wrote at the beginning? About you being amazing. If you've followed everything in the book and are feeling the benefits, then you will be able to take my compliment. After all, you have left an abusive relationship and recognised much of what was unhealthy about that relationship and the coping strategies you had to adopt during that time. Picking up this book is part of your healing process. Well done, you are amazing.

Sue Penna

CONTACTS

Below is a list of organisations who you can contact if you want help. They will signpost you to your local agencies.

Freephone National Domestic Abuse Helpline
0808 200 0247
www.nationaldahelpline.org.uk

Women's Aid
www.womensaid.org.uk
info@womensaid.org.uk

Galop (for lesbian, gay, bisexual and transgender people)
0800 999 5428
www.galop.org.uk

Rape Crisis (England and Wales)
0808 802 9999
www.rapecrisis.org.uk

Scotland's Domestic Abuse and Forced Marriage Helpline
0800 027 1234
www.sdafmh.org.uk

Scottish Women's Aid
0131 226 6606
www.scottishwomensaid.org.uk

Wales Domestic Abuse Helpline
0808 80 10 800
www.allwaleshelpline.org.uk

Women's Aid Federation (Northern Ireland)
0800 917 1414
www.womensaidni.org

Welsh Women's Aid / Cymorth i Ferched Cymru
0808 80 10 800
www.welshwomensaid.org.uk

Men's Advice Line
0808 801 0327
www.mensadviceline.org.uk

Acknowledgements

I'd like to thank the following people for their help, guidance and support in writing this book. My colleagues at Rockpool, Jo Majauskis, Vashti Wickers, Laura Harris and Kirsty Passmore Mooney.

I'd also like to say a big thank you to Jennifer Gilmour, who supplied me with her amazing observations and gave permission to use them in this book.

Also, Mark Pugh, my editor and publishing adviser.

Sue Penna has worked with individuals who have psychological trauma for over 30 years in her professional life as a clinician, trainer and supervisor both within the NHS and independently. She has specialised in writing psycho-educational programmes that promote trauma-informed practice and a recovery model.

Sue is the co-founder of Rock Pool CIC, where she is the Chief Creative Officer and heads a team of sector experts in designing and delivering trauma-informed training and recovery programmes.

Sue has an extensive background in the domestic abuse sector and devised the Recovery Toolkit programme, on which this book is based, which was the first trauma-informed programme for individuals who had experienced abuse in the UK. For more information about the work of Sue and Rock Pool CIC, please check out the company website: www.rockpool.life

Jennifer Gilmour is an advocate for women and an author. Jennifer has published two books, Isolation Junction and Clipped Wings. For more information about Jennifer check out her website: www.jennifergilmour.com

Mark Pugh is a writer, journalist, audiobook producer and publisher. For information about print and digital publishing or audiobook production, please email markpugh@email.com

SOURCES AND PERMISSIONS

Definition
1 Taken from www.gov.uk/government/news/new-definition-of-domestic-violence accessed on 14th February 2020

2 The UK government's reason that this definition only references those aged 16 and over is to avoid the risk of "blurring the line between domestic abuse and child abuse". Taken from the 'Statutory Definition of Domestic Abuse Fact Sheet (updated 1 November 2019)'.

Week Two   Dynamics Of Domestic Abuse
3 Graham, Dee LR, 'Loving to Survive' Published by New York University Press (1994)

4 Biderman's Cycle of Coercive Control - Originally published as part of Methods of Interrogation and Indoctrination. Presented by the New York Academy of Medicine and based on the research and development program of the Air Force Personnel and Training Research Center. Lackland Air Force Base, Texas. Used with permission ©United States Government

Week Three   Self-Esteem
5 The Universal Declaration of Human Rights (1948), United Nations

6 Beattie, Melody, 'Codependent No More – How to stop controlling others and Start Caring for Yourself ', Published by Hazelden, 1986

7 Rosemberg, Morris. 1989. Society and the Adolescent Self-Image. Revised edition. Middletown, CT: Wesleyan University Press.

8 Based on: Tomlinson, D, & Slater, D, 'Depression' Published by Routledge 2003 p73

Week Four   How We Cope Emotionally

9 Domestic Violence among Female Psychiatric Patients by John F. Morgan, Senior Lecturer in Psychiatry, Leeds, and St George's University, London, Gabriella Zolese, Consultant Psychiatrist, South West London and St George's Mental Health NHS Trust, Jane McNulty, Consultant Psychiatrist, Sussex Partnership NHS Trust, and Sharon Gebhardt, Consultant Psychiatrist, Surrey and Borders Partnership NHS Trust.

10 Ibid

11 Staff Burnout, Volume 1, National Drug Abuse Center (U.S) 1980

Week Six   Self-Care

12 Falk et al., 2015; Cascio et al., 2016
accessed via www.positivepsychology.com 14th February 2020

Week Seven   A New Assertive You

13 Cambridge English Dictionary online. www.dictionary.cambridge.org Accessed 8th January 2020

14 Dryden, W, "Assertiveness Step by Step", published by Sheldon Press 2004

Week Ten   Grief And Loss

15 Kübler-Ross E, 'On Death and Dying'. Routledge 1969

Week Eleven Healthy Relationships

16 Messina, James "Tools for Relationships - Handling Intimacy", published by Kendall Hunt 1991

Manufactured by Amazon.ca
Bolton, ON

13238164R00085